The New Workforce Challenge

This page intentionally left blank

The New Workforce Challenge
How Today's Leading Companies Are Adapting to the Future

Andrés Hatum

© Andrés Hatum 2013

Softcover reprint of the hardcover 1st edition 2013 978-1-137-30298-4

All rights reserved. No reproduction, copy or transmission of this publication may be made without written permission.

No portion of this publication may be reproduced, copied or transmitted save with written permission or in accordance with the provisions of the Copyright, Designs and Patents Act 1988, or under the terms of any licence permitting limited copying issued by the Copyright Licensing Agency, Saffron House, 6–10 Kirby Street, London EC1N 8TS.

Any person who does any unauthorized act in relation to this publication may be liable to criminal prosecution and civil claims for damages.

The author has asserted his right to be identified as the author of this work in accordance with the Copyright, Designs and Patents Act 1988.

First published 2013 by
PALGRAVE MACMILLAN

Palgrave Macmillan in the UK is an imprint of Macmillan Publishers Limited, registered in England, company number 785998, of Houndmills, Basingstoke, Hampshire RG21 6XS.

Palgrave Macmillan in the US is a division of St Martin's Press LLC, 175 Fifth Avenue, New York, NY 10010.

Palgrave Macmillan is the global academic imprint of the above companies and has companies and representatives throughout the world.

Palgrave® and Macmillan® are registered trademarks in the United States, the United Kingdom, Europe and other countries.

ISBN 978-1-349-45403-7   ISBN 978-1-137-30299-1 (eBook)
DOI 10.1007/978-1-137-30299-1

This book is printed on paper suitable for recycling and made from fully managed and sustained forest sources. Logging, pulping and manufacturing processes are expected to conform to the environmental regulations of the country of origin.

A catalogue record for this book is available from the British Library.

A catalog record for this book is available from the Library of Congress.

10 9 8 7 6 5 4 3 2 1
22 21 20 19 18 17 16 15 14 13

Contents

Figures and Tables vii
Acknowledgments xi

	Introduction	1
1	**Organizing and the New Agile and Virtual Firm**	**11**
	New Ways of Organizing: The Rise of Complexity	11
	The Agile and Virtual Firm	21
	Case in Point: Open Business Model at elBulli	31
2	**Demographic Changes in the Workplace**	**35**
	Different Generations and Perspectives	35
	The Millennial Generation: "We Are Going to Rock the Workplace"	43
	Are Generations Similar Worldwide? India, China and the West	50
	Case in Point: Frisse Blikken (Fresh Forces), New Organizational Paradigms for New Talent	58
3	**Attracting Millennials to the Workplace**	**63**
	Building the Employee Value Proposition (EVP) to Attract Millennials	63
	New Ways of Recruiting: The Role of Social Networks	81

	Case in Point: "Reveal" by L'Oréal, Attracting Millennials and Guiding Them into the Workplace	95
4	**New Learning Paradigms and the Challenge of Developing the Future Leaders**	**99**
	The New Paradigms of Learning	99
	Developing the Next Generation of Leaders	112
	Topsy Turvy: Careers Reloaded	127
	Case in Point: La Masía–Barcelona Club – A Talent Development School for the Future	141
5	**The New Realignment Contract**	**145**
	In Search of … Agility	145
	Concluding Remarks	161
	Interviews	165
	Notes	169
	Bibliography	183
	Index of Companies and Organizations	193
	Subject Index	195

Figures and Tables

Figures

1.1	Business model at Wikipedia	15
1.2	Business model at Threadless.com	15
1.3	Features of an agile and virtual organization	26
1.4	Open business model at elBulli	33
2.1	Millennials in the agile and virtual firm	44
2.2	Organizational scope over time and across generations	49
3.1	Deloitte's Leadership Academy	73
3.2	Faster, freer and further: EVP at Coty	76
3.3	Getting strategic about attracting Millennials: Recruiting process at Sodexo	85
3.4	Finding the right set of benefits for each generation	88
4.1	Learning strategy matrix	106
4.2	Learning experience for Millennials	111
4.3	Leaders of the future	114
4.4	Development activities according to their learning and collaboration impact	119
4.5	Developing managerial and interpersonal competencies	120
4.6	An example of a career ladder	129
4.7	An approach toward a customized portfolio career (CPC): Richard's case	136

4.8	An approach toward a CPC: Anika's case	137
4.9	An integrated process: Developing talent at FC Barcelona	144
5.1	7-S framework (based on Peters and Waterman, 1982)	146
5.2	Nine elements of organizational health (based on Keller and Price, 2011)	148
5.3	A model of organizational agility	149
5.4	Creating scenarios to anticipate the future (based on Butterfield, 2006)	152
5.5	Aligning the organization and the new HR paradigm	155
5.6	Natura's alignment model	155
5.7	A model of change and stability for the future organization	159
5.8	A model of organizing for the future workplace and workforce	161

Tables

I.1	Practices, processes and organizations (relevant examples)	5
I.2	Cases in point	7
1.1	Evolution of organizations over time and technological revolution	18
1.2	Properties associated with agile and virtual firms	27
2.1	Main features throughout different generations	39
2.2	Inside the different generations: The differences	40
2.3	Implications of Millennials' characteristics	48
3.1	EVP dimensions supporting Millennials' characteristics	75
4.1	Millennials' characteristics and the learning process	103

4.2	Future leadership competencies	116
4.3	Managerial competencies and Millennials' characteristics	123
4.5	Millennials' characteristics and implications for careers and organizations	132

This page intentionally left blank

Acknowledgments

The first thing I do when I start reading a book is to read the acknowledgments: who the author has thanked, trusted and relied on. This window into the writer's influences, in my opinion, provides important insights into the author's soul.

I want to thank first of all my students, from whom I receive constant enthusiasm in exchange for imparting knowledge in the classroom. My students do not realize how important they have been, and will continue be, to me. It is my students who make me passionate about teaching.

To my mentor, friend and "maestro," Professor Andrew Pettigrew, to whom I am indebted for life. He guided me on the path to my professional identity. His support, time investment and patience cannot be sufficiently acknowledged.

To my friends Lorenzo Preve, Javier Quintanilla and Maví Zingoni, who are always close to me no matter the distance.

To Santiago García Belmonte, Lucía Christello, Ezequiel Garbers and Guillermina Galián, whose friendship and monthly discussions add much joy to my life.

To Adriana Urquía, who supports me whenever I need assistance and with whom I enjoy working very much.

To Patricio Farcuh, whose friendship and generosity at the CIGRA research center at IAE Business School have been of great value to me.

To Brenda Priebke who helped me to enhance the first draft of my book. To my editor, Eleanor Davey-Corrigan, thanks for the trust invested in me again! and for your kind help throughout the process of publishing the book. Thanks to you and your team: Hannah Fox and Mritunjai Sahai.

To my mother, who left us a few years ago but whose teaching and experience survive and are being passed on to younger generations in my family. I had in my mother a rare combination of experienced wise advisor and close friend. My mother taught me the importance of a job well done and of following one's passion. I dedicate this book to her constant love and support. One day we will reunite with all the books I wrote with her support, and we will read them together, promise!

I finally dedicate this book to my wife Gabriela and my children Nicolás, Sofía and Victoria. They are the stars who light up my life. To them, thank you for being the source of my inspiration and drive.

Introduction

> I never predict. I just look out the window and see what's visible – but not yet seen.
>
> Peter Drucker[1]

In attempting to understand the impact of new generations in the workplace, I found a vast volume of literature detailing the pros and cons of incorporating the young Millennials, a generation noted for its caprices and technological savvy, into the workforce.

Most of the books that I found on this subject simply provide descriptions of the new generation. Of course this information is important: We need to know the strengths, weaknesses and motivations of the new wave of entrants into the workforce, as this new wave will shape the future organization. But is this information enough to anticipate and prepare for the future challenges that will be imposed by this generation of workers?

Many previous generations have entered the workforce over time, and these earlier generations also presented challenges for organizations. However, firms were generally able to absorb these new entrants into their organizations and build new capabilities for the future. If this were the case presently, I would start and finish my book right here. However, I found that firms are facing a new challenge: The new generation is getting its space within organizations, but organizations are changing faster than they ever did before. This new territory makes the future a tricky place for many currently successful firms. It would thus be a mistake to think that organizations will be shaped by Millennials only – indeed, organizations are being shaped by the turbulent context in which companies worldwide are immersed.

Organizations are taking different forms and shapes as never seen before. Shedding light on recent changes that organizations have gone through and additional changes likely to come in the future will help us understand how to manage the new workforce entering companies. In particular, this understanding will allow companies to not only adapt their paradigms with respect to how to manage new generations but also design new ways to organize such that they can successfully respond to a dynamic, changeable external environment. It is this understanding that will allow managers to build the future firm in which the younger generation will be easily included and succeed.

Notice that organizing and managing the new young workforce are not separate processes. The different organizational forms that companies have adopted throughout history (e.g., functional, matrix and divisional structures) were complemented by people from different generations (e.g., traditionalists, baby boomers, Gen Xers and Millennials or Gen Yers). Firms have moved forward by adapting to both a changing external environment and internal demographic transformations over time.

What makes this time so different from before? There has been always change. However, we are witnessing a rapid transformation of how companies organize at the same time a new generation is taking over critical jobs. This new generation is shaping organizational life, but organizations are also bringing deep renovations that aim to adapt to the environment.

Turbulence and *turmoil* are words that are becoming common after the financial crisis of 2008–2009, not only for less developed countries but also for all countries. In this context, the challenge of organizations is to find the best way to survive and, at the same time, incorporate new generations within it.

This book aims to help companies meet the above challenge by examining how firms are organizing for the future and the impact of the new organizational forms on the workplace as well as the practices that firms are putting into place to attract, develop and retain the new generation of workers. By shedding light on the new forms of organizing and the way firms adapt to the external environment, this book will allow managers to consider how their firm can incorporate the new workforce. Moreover, by identifying features characterizing the new workforce, this book will allow companies to adapt their practices and review their structure so as to be able to accommodate the new generation.

I strongly believe that both the workplace and the workforce need to be analyzed together to be able to see the big picture and avoid superficial analysis of trends or fads. In doing so, I expect to be able to look out the window, as Drucker suggested in the quote that leads this book, and understand what is driving the changes at the organizational and human levels.

Analyzes of the workforce and the workplace are not new. However, these two topics have not been previously considered together. A number of factors simultaneously impact the workforce and the workplace. Technological changes, for example, are having this double impact due to the importance of increasing technological capability as well as the surge in social networks and participation in organizations. Demographic changes are also influencing both the workforce and organizations – not only is the ascendance of Gen Y influencing the workplace but also the increasing longevity and productivity of the workforce is also putting firms worldwide under the enormous challenge of stretching careers.

In line with the view that the workforce and workplace should be analyzed together, Gratton (2011) has recently documented the changes the workplace is going through and underscored how critical the workforce, that is, people, are to a firm's success in this context. She highlights three critical dark sides to the future of work: fragmentation, isolation and exclusion. Fragmentation implies an increase in the variety of activities one faces during the day, which results in a decrease in one's ability to concentrate and capacity to learn. Isolation implies the loss of physical contact in the workplace and the emergence of internet-based interaction. Finally, exclusion at the workplace implies an increase in status, anxiety and shame.

All of these changes require significant changes in paradigms and real organizational transformation to be able to adapt to the new world ahead. Gary Hamel (2007) believes that the successful management going into the future will require innovation. He is bewildered at how the world and technology have changed so much, and how people have transformed their lives accordingly, yet at the same time most organizations are lagging behind in terms of the changes needed to adapt and survive. That is, he sees a contradiction between the huge transformations in people and capabilities, on the one hand, and the reality of organizations, on the other. As he puts it, "so here we are: still working on Taylor-type puzzles and living in Weber-type organizations" (Hamel, 2007: 14). The future of the workforce and of the workplace is full of incredible opportunities, however, and thus organizations need to find the courage to renew themselves, bringing in the best people to support them.

This book is aimed at managers, students and academics alike. Managers will find thoughtful discussions on trends in organizational structure as well as on innovative practices to attract, develop and commit the new, young workforce. Academics will find information on new forms of organizing and managing. Finally, students in MBA or management programs will obtain theoretical knowledge and practical understanding of what firms are doing today to align their organization and workforce with the new environmental challenges.

In addition to presenting the theoretical underpinnings behind the different trends and practices discussed in this book, case studies from real companies and organizations are presented. Table I.1 summarizes the most important practices and processes considered in this book and the associated case studies that are incorporated to illustrate a given practice or process.

Each chapter ends with a case study ("Case in Point"). Each case study is selected according to the following criteria: First, it should be representative of the theme discussed in the chapter; second, it should be able to offer a compelling description of the theme as it is performed in the organization (i.e., we need to have good access to information within the chosen firm). Table I.2 summarizes the Cases in Point presented in this book.

Many other firms are referred to in the book to illustrate specific situations or practices, or to provide examples of clear

Table I.1 *Practices, processes and organizations (relevant examples)*

Topic and chapter	Companies	Industries	Countries
Crowdsourcing – Chapter 1	Wikipedia	Online encyclopedia	United States
	Threadless	Online design	United States
	Innocentive	Online scientific service	United States
Generations worldwide – Chapter 2	ASIAM Business Group*	Manufacturing and quality control processes, textile industry	China
Work and life integration – Chapter 2	Cirque du Soleil	Entertainment	Canada
Aging workforce – Chapter 2	BMW	Car manufacturer	Germany
Employee value proposition (EVP) – Chapter 3	Coty*	Cosmetics	France
Dimensions of EVP – Chapter 3	AES*	Power and energy	United States
	Teach for America	NGO education	United States
	Salesforce.com	Software	United States
	Peace Corps	NGO	United States
	SAP*	Software	United States
	Deloitte*	Consulting	United States
	Accenture	Consulting	United States

(*continued*)

Table I.1 *Continued*

Topic and chapter	Companies	Industries	Countries
Recruitment strategies for Millennials – Chapter 3	L'Oréal*	Cosmetics	France
	Sodexo	Food service and facility management	France
	AMC Theatres	Theaters	United States
	Zappo	Online shoe retailer	United States
	Cliff Bar & Co	Organic bars	United States
	Dow*	Chemical	United States
	McDonald's	Fast food	United States
New learning paradigms – Chapter 4	BP	Oil and energy	United Kingdom
	Lastminute.com*	Online travel and leisure retailer	United Kingdom
Developing future leaders – Chapter 4	Rabobank*	Banking	The Netherlands
	Pernod Ricard*	Wine and spirit producer	France
Careers – Chapter 4	Accordion Partners*	Investment consulting	United States
A model of organizational agility – Chapter 5	Best Buy	Electronic retailer	United States
	Natura*	Beauty	Brazil
	AGD*	Farming and oil producer	Argentina

*Case written by the author to illustrate relevant the practice or process. The other cases come from public information sources.

Table I.2 *Cases in point*

Chapter	Topic	Case in point	Industry	Country
Chapter 1: Organizing and the new agile and virtual firm	Open business model	elBulli	Gastronomy	Spain
Chapter 2: Demographic changes in the workplace	New organizational paradigms for new talent	Frisse Blikken	Service, consultancy	The Netherlands
Chapter 3: Attracting Millennials to the workplace	Attracting Millennials and guiding them into the workplace	L'Oréal	Beauty, cosmetics	France
Chapter 4: New learning paradigms and the challenge of developing the future leaders	Developing younger generations for long-term commitment	FC Barcelona, La Masía	Sports	Spain

executions of certain processes. Such references, however, are concise and are used simply to shed light on very specific topics covered in the book.

Two different sections will be found in each chapter. First, sections called "Future Trends" provide interviews with experts from different fields studied in this book. These experts provided brief opinions about diverse issues of relevance to the chapter at hand. Second, sections called "The Unresolved Challenge" draw attention to critical issues for the future of organizations and employees alike, such as the dichotomy between increased virtuality and disaggregated jobs, the role of older generations at work, the problems related to commitment to the workplace over the long term, and the challenges posed by lattice and ladder organizations. All of these unresolved issues, as they are referred to in this book, are challenges that firms will face as we look to the future.

Chapter 1 begins by providing a discussion of the different approaches toward the new ways of organizing. In particular, it describes the theoretical underpinnings and evolution of new organizational arrangements, such as open business models and crowdsourcing, and it discusses the role of social networks in the way firms organize. By knowing the different organizational forms that have emerged, the reader will be better able to understand the evolution of organizational structures, that is, of how firms have responded to the various hurdles that they have confronted depending on the context in which they are embedded – a complex environment that in recent years has been shaped by jolts and turbulence due not only to hypercompetition but also to crisis.

Next, the chapter introduces and develops the concept of the agile and virtual firm. This is an attempt to summarize the new trends observed in practice. It aims to reinforce the idea that firms need to think outside the box in terms of their organizational structures. In doing so, it analyzes the individual and organizational determinants of organizational agility as well as the main characteristics of agile firms.

Chapter 2 considers the future workforce. While Chapter 1 focuses on the challenges that organizations face in terms of adapting and organizing, Chapter 2 focuses on the changes occurring in the workforce. This chapter begins by clarifying the differences between the different generations at work (i.e., traditionalists, baby boomers, Gen Xers and Millennials or Gen Yers). It then describes the challenges associated with the overlapping generations working together, and the specific characteristics associated with the Millennials generation, for instance, the importance they attach to multitasking, technology, integrating life and work, and social awareness. Millennials have been exposed to a wider organizational scope than ever, and as a result Millennials' characteristics may help firms transform themselves in the era of virtuality.

Chapter 2 also devotes a short section to generational differences and similarities worldwide with an emphasis on India and China, to underscore the point that managers need to be careful to adapt organizational strategies and practices according to the country in which the company is operating. It also raises the issue of the aging workforce, which will affect countries and companies alike into the future.

Chapter 3 focuses on how to attract Millennials. This generation's multitasking aptitude, value on integrating work and life, social awareness and technological savvy are viewed through the lens of identifying the employee value proposition (EVP) dimensions used to attract Millennials. These dimensions are the social impact of the job, the windscreen to the world and the "me brand."

Once the basis of an attractive EVP for Millennials has been identified, the chapter turns to how current and future organizations should recruit Millennials. Three strategies (with complementary examples) are examined: the importance of being social (i.e., the role of social networks), the significance of being aggressively persuasive about the benefits the company has to offer and the new role of organizations in coaching candidates. The three strategies can be adopted altogether.

Chapter 4 tackles an issue of particular importance for new generations and organizations alike: new paradigms of learning and the development of future leaders. This chapter begins by laying out the dichotomy between how learning has changed over time, on the one hand, and the inertia in some processes such as teaching, on the other. It emphasizes the need for companies to transform and update some of their knowledge transfer and mentoring processes. To do so, a new teaching strategy is required whereby the workplace is where part of the learning process takes place. Individual learning, social learning, self-management and learning led by the organization are each analyzed as part of the overall strategy.

It turns next to the development of the next generation of leaders. Developing future leaders is not only important but also indispensable for the long-term sustainability of organizations. Two dimensions are deemed critical in the development of future leaders: the capacity for learning, unlearning and renewal, and the ability to collaborate. This chapter proposes a set of competencies for future leaders, a group of activities for their development and some competencies for today's managers who face the challenge of developing the future leaders.

Chapter 4 also analyzes future careers in the context of the organizational changes that firms will be required to make in the future. Concepts such as boundaryless careers, flexible work, portfolio career and mass career customization are reviewed, and a new perspective of careers that takes into account the fact that firms will have to adapt to the new generation's development needs is proposed. I call this career perspective *customized portfolio career*.

The final chapter, Chapter 5, returns to the topic of how firms organize and introduce a model of organizational agility in which elements of organizing and managing are relevant for the future workplace and workforce. It proposes four determinants of organizational agility that impact the dimensions previously mentioned: new cognitive diversity, fast anticipatory capacity, new HR paradigms and a strong sense of purpose. These four determinants affect the four elements that capture a firm's innovation, responsiveness, coherence and alignment, factors that are critical for the survival and success of the organization into the future. Some concluding remarks end the book.

1
Organizing and the New Agile and Virtual Firm

NEW WAYS OF ORGANIZING: THE RISE OF COMPLEXITY

Malone (2004), trying to understand changes in organizational patterns over time, concludes that businesses have been structured according to the way in which societies have been organized. He notes that until 1800 most businesses worldwide were family firms that enjoyed a lot of freedom but rarely interacted with members of other groups. Corporate hierarchies emerged in 1870 with the railroad industry, which was one of the first to embrace centralization. The benefits of scale were important to the realization of the centralization process. Malone highlights the case of Ford, where the amount of time to make a Model T had dropped from 12 hours and 8 minutes to only 1 hour and 33 minutes in 1913. Many companies that could not achieve such scale benefits did not survive. Adaptation was clearly necessary to survival.

While early corporations were single-product firms, the same companies started to expand into new product areas at the beginning of the twentieth century (Chandler, 1990). The resulting increase in complexity required new organizational forms. Business units and the multidivisional corporation emerged as a way to support the multiproduct, multi-business strategy.

The foregoing organizational model faced a crisis in the 1980s when *ing* processes – outsourcing, delayering and rightsizing, among other ways of adjusting and reshaping the organization – were implemented in an effort to survive the turmoil of the 1980s. During this period, historically large and successful corporations suffered from cutbacks and inertia. At the same time, however, start-up firms and the new venture capital sector that emerged in Silicon Valley developed new ways of organizing in which leanness and agility were favored over the traditional hierarchical approaches (Malone et al., 2003). As these new ways of organizing became more widely adopted, the resulting tendency toward decentralization had a large impact on the way firms are organized today: Today's firms are flatter and leaner, with less reliance on hierarchies designed to manage a highly centralized organization. Adaptation was thus again necessary to be able to face a hypercompetitive environment characterized by huge transformations within corporations and the need to anticipate changes and develop new innovations to bring to market.

So what makes it possible for organizations to adapt rapidly to external changes? How can organizations learn to adapt to volatile conditions? Concepts such as the flexible firm (Hatum, 2007; Volberda, 1999), the innovative firm (Blau and McKinley, 1979; Drucker, 1999; Pettigrew and Fenton, 2000), the adaptive firm (Haeckel, 1999) or the agile firm (Goldman et al., 1995) have been proposed in an effort to explain the organizational capabilities needed to allow firms to adjust to an ever-changing environment.

Grantham (2000) emphasizes the importance of the "Hollywood" model of organization for the future. To produce a feature-length film, hundreds of small firms and individuals coalesce around a project that is led by a team of producers and directors. Talent from one film may work together on future films. But when a particular project is complete, the virtual organization that was created comes to an end. This model allows for maximum flexibility, but it also leads to minimum loyalty and endless jockeying for advantage.[2]

Hedlund (1994) introduces the concept of the N-form, which is based on different elements of an ideal organization, for instance, lateral rather than vertical communication, temporary constellations of people and units rather than permanent structures, and heterarchy rather than hierarchy. Hedlund's N-form might have been seen as futuristic at the time he predicted this type of organization to be on the horizon. However, as we will see later, the new forms of organizing observed in practice today are not far from this idea. Similarly, based on an analysis of the complexities of the four-pillar organization structure at Procter & Gamble (P&G) and the six-dimensional organizational structure of IBM, Galbraith (2009) predicts a fragmentation of the business environment and the adoption of a dimensional matrix structure consisting of functions, business units and geographies.

One of the most recent empirical attempts to understand the ways firms organize in an effort to adapt to changing competitive contexts comes from Pettigrew et al. (2003). Instead of focusing on ideal ways of organizing, Pettigrew and his colleagues focus on how firms organize in reality and examine the indicators of firms' organizational choices. The conclusion of their international survey is that the most adaptable and innovative firms have combined changes in structure (i.e., more decentralization, delayering and project forms of organizing) with changes in processes (i.e., horizontal communication, investments in information technology and new human resource (HR) practices) and changes in firm boundaries (i.e., downscoping, outsourcing and more strategic alliances).

Pettigrew et al.'s research sheds light on the new ways of organizing and on trends companies should consider when restructuring themselves to be able to successfully compete during times of high complexity. In short, it appears that successful and adaptable organizations will need to support high levels of decentralized participation, rely less on undifferentiated formal organization and compete more through their informal uniqueness. In line with this view, the open business model is emerging as one way to thrive in the context of a hypercompetitive business environment. In contrast to a traditional closed office, the open business model involves sharing resources with competitors (in ways that do not put the firm at a competitive disadvantage) and being open to new ideas from almost any source. Sandulli and Chesbrough (2009) and Chesbrough (2006) point to the importance of both the seller's and buyer's perspectives within this model. The buyer's perspective allows firms to incorporate resources from other firms in their own business model. The seller's perspective, however, allows the resources of one firm to be used in another company.

The open business model is starting to supersede traditional ways of structuring firms, including functional, matrix, divisional or business unit designs, which are increasingly insufficient to confront the jolts and turmoil characterizing today's dynamic environment. One of the largest open business model initiatives currently in existence is Google's Android platform, the first open source mobile phone platform brought to market.[3] As an open source project, anyone can contribute to Android and influence its direction. Google understands that in exchange for giving up a certain amount of control, it can gain tremendous benefits from receiving participation and ideas from around the world.

Crowdsourcing is another new way firms can increase their access to great ideas and talent. Jeff Howe, author of the book *Crowdsourcing* (2008), defines it as "the act of taking a job traditionally performed by a designated agent (usually an employee) and outsourcing it to an undefined, generally large group of people in the form of an open call."[4] Howe acknowledges that while "crowdsourcing" encourages comparison with "outsourcing" and its negative impact on employment, the practice allows firms to obtain access to top talent from around the world and thereby deliver a high-quality, reliable product at a competitive price.

Not all models of crowdsourcing, however, bear the same degree of complexity (see Figures 1.1 and 1.2). Consider first the case of Wikipedia (http://www.wikipedia.org/). Since its creation in 2001, Wikipedia has rapidly grown into one of the world's largest reference websites, attracting nearly 78 million visitors monthly as of January 2010. This growth has been based on content provided largely by anonymous internet volunteers who collaborate to write and update content without pay. As of October 2012, Wikipedia

Organizing and the New Agile and Virtual Firm

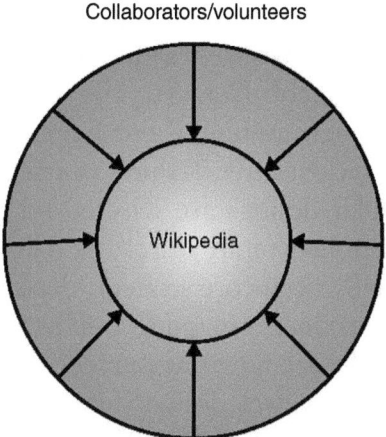

Figure 1.1 *Business model at Wikipedia*

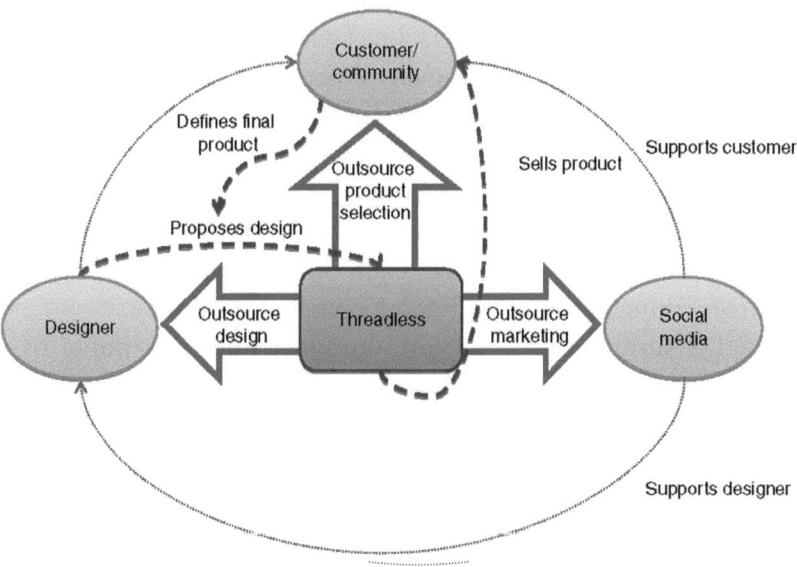

Figure 1.2 *Business model at Threadless.com*

counts more than 77,000 active contributors working on more than 22,000,000 articles in 285 languages.[5]

Figure 1.1 summarizes the relatively simple business model of Wikipedia, where the contributions of volunteer collaborators are key to the organization's success.

A more complex model of crowdsourcing can be found in the case of Threadless (http://www.threadless.com), launched in 2000 by Jake Nickell and Jacob DeHart. The idea is simple: Artists submit a T-shirt design, potential consumers vote for the best design, the winner receives free T-shirts bearing his or her design and the most popular designs are selected for printing and sale by the Threadless online retail store.[6] At Threadless, decisions that have traditionally been core strategic decisions of firms – the design of potential products offered as well as the choice of which products will be sold – are now outsourced.

Today, Threadless receives design submissions from a worldwide community of more than 80,000 artists and participation from a community of over 1.3 million members who vote regularly on their favorite design submissions. Threadless further boasts over 1.5 million followers on Twitter and 100,000 fans on Facebook.[7] Thus, by engaging customers, understanding what interests them and building on this information, this 50-person company harnessed the power of social networks and consumer support to grow its revenues to over US$30 million a year. Indeed, as cofounder Jack Nickell observes, "the best brands are built from a community of people who make each other realize they share a love for something. They're built from something genuine."[8]

Figure 1.2 summarizes the more complex business model of Threadless, where virtuality, networks and social media play key roles.

If Threadless has created a new kind of marketplace for products, InnoCentive (http://www.innocentive.com) has done so for ideas. InnoCentive is a website that allows people and companies to collaborate in solving scientific and business challenges, something previously hard to imagine as firms have traditionally kept research and development innovations to themselves. The company distinguishes *seekers* and *solvers*. Seekers receive help from the company in defining their problem, writing their challenge statement and evaluating possible solutions. Solvers may be professionals, retired scientists, students or anyone who can answer a problem that has stumped a company's own researchers. Cash rewards are sometimes offered to those who solve a challenge, with award amounts having ranged from US$5,000 to US$1 million.⁹

InnoCentive, based in Waltham, Massachusetts, began as an in-house resource where research scientists at Eli Lilly & Co. could go to help one another. Now it is independent, with Indianapolis-based Lilly a founding shareholder. By opening the website's reach beyond its own research and development team, Lilly gains access to a large number of individuals and companies that may have ideas that can be of value to the company. At the same time, InnoCentive provides an important problem-solving service that delivers solutions to approximately 40% of the challenges that are posed.[10] Clients using InnoCentive include, among others, P&G, Solvay, Eli Lilly & Co. and Oil Spill Recovery Institute.[11]

The word *revolution* can be used to characterize the change that organizations experience over time. In recent years, firms have witnessed a technological revolution that increasingly erodes company boundaries. For instance, the social network boom connects companies directly to the outside world with few, if any, filters "managing the message." The impact of such changes has led to ways of organizing that differ radically from those seen before, which begs us to think about the deep transformations that firms have been going through.

Table 1.1 summarizes the upheaval that firms have confronted since the dot-com boom and more recently the emergence of social networks. The table shows clearly that while organizational design evolved slowly between 1950 and the early 1990s, the advance of the internet and the growth in social networks have led companies to accelerate the pace with which they develop new ways of organizing. Mark Zuckerberg, in response to questions about Facebook's effect on society, stated that "[w]hen there is more openness, with everyone being able to express their opinion very quickly, more of the economy starts to operate like a fit economy. It puts the onus on companies and organizations to be more good, and more trustworthy."[12] When an organization has to confront many social networks and the rapid development of new internet tools, the openness that Zuckerberg refers to is even bigger for every firm.

Table 1.1 Evolution of organizations over time and technological revolution

	1950s–1960s	1970s–1980s	1990s	2000 to present	The future?
Evolution of organization design	Bureaucratic form/ functional form	Matrix form	Network form	Social networks	
Dot-com evolution	UCLA creates Arpanet, the beginning of the internet	E-commerce (ATM and telephone banking)	Online e-commerce Amazon Yahoo eBay MSM Google	Dot-com collapse Wikipedia PayPal	Virtual and agile firm
Social networks launch			Six Degrees Live Journal	Fotolog LinkedIn MySpace Hi5 Flickr Facebook YouTube Twitter	

The terms *agility* and *virtuality* well capture attributes that companies will need to cultivate in order to successfully respond to the challenges they will face in the near future. Agile and virtual firms will shape the marketplace and at the same time will both influence and be influenced by the new workforce. In short, the increased use of new organizational structures, such as open business models and crowdsourcing that we introduced in this chapter, in addition to the widespread use of social media will continue to change the way we work in the future.

What are the main features of the virtual and agile firms of the future? The next section attempts to briefly identify the main characteristics of the agile and virtual firm, and the organizational and managerial determinants needed for such a firm to arise.

The Unresolved Challenge: Virtual People and Disaggregated Jobs

> There was a time in which people arrived to the office, sat at a desk, complied with a work week and established relationships with their colleagues. The work environment is changing, however. The workplace is becoming virtual, with employees working anywhere, anytime. These employees are able to work in a community of "virtual" colleagues and customers located in different parts of the world. Thanks to technological advances they can work in real time. There is no doubt that technology is providing employees a new level of flexibility.
>
> The disaggregation and virtualization of jobs have been spotted by McKinsey Global Institute (MGI) (see Manyka et al., 2011) as trends associated with the changing nature of the workplace. Disaggregation of jobs implies the creation of more specialized jobs. As the Manyka et al. (2011: 47) study suggests, "It is no longer about one person doing ten tasks, it's more like ten people contributing to one

function, each with a specialized task." Thus, disaggregation will create new, highly specialized jobs. Quam (2010) suggests that disaggregation is a consequence of new work configurations (such as modularization and new work designs) and new ways to organize employees (such as self-organized workgroups and freelance teams).

Virtualization, however, allows people to work anywhere, anytime with higher motivation, low levels of turnover and even higher productivity. Employees can be assigned to multiple teams at the same time, and dynamic team membership can allow people to move from one project to another. The cost savings associated with the reduced need for dedicated office space and other infrastructure for everyone, and with the efficiencies that the new technologies are bringing in, mean that outsourcing is likely to increasingly occur at the intracountry level instead of simply involving the transfer of work abroad to cheaper labor in less developed countries.

Virtual workplaces and disaggregated jobs may translate into firms hiring a larger proportion of highly skilled employees than they could if they hired only where their office is located. These trends may also translate into firms hiring a larger proportion of its employees on a part-time basis. These possibilities raise important questions. For example, in the future, will people be able to say that they have held a full-time job at some point over the course of their professional lives? Furthermore, how will people working in virtual, disaggregated positions be trained, and will they be taken into consideration for managerial positions within the company, or will they become a special cast of skilled nonmanagement employees?

At the managerial level, virtualization and disaggregation imply several challenges for senior management and middle managers alike. First, these trends require a high level of coordination to make sure that results are still achieved. Second, these changes require a greater level of communication and collaboration. Finally, for middle managers these trends imply a different approach toward managing employees that might not be geographically proximate but rather far away. The ability to manage remotely and reassign tasks dynamically across a network will increasingly be competencies that a manager will need to count on to be successful.

Ideas at a Glance

New Ways of Organizing

- New ways of organizing, such as open business models or crowdsourcing, have emerged and are superseding traditional structures.

- Open business models share resources from the organization with competitors and bring resources from the market to the organization.

- Crowdsourcing expands the traditional practice of outsourcing to undefined, large groups.

- Social networks are being incorporated into the new ways of organizing.

THE AGILE AND VIRTUAL FIRM

What Does Being Agile Mean?

Different definitions of agility share some common features that can distinguish it from other concepts. Characteristics or dimensions associated with agility include the ability to take advantage of opportunities (Baker, 1998; Dove, 1995; Dyer and Shafer, 2003; Shafer, 1999), the ability to respond to unpredictable or unforeseen situations (Campbell, 1998; Dove, 1995; Goldman et al., 1995; Goranson, 1999; Grantham et al., 2007; Ward, 1994) and the ability to succeed and be profitable at the end of the day (Dove, 1995; Goldman et al., 1995; Goranson, 1999; Hugos, 2009; Ward, 1994).

What is *organizational agility* then; how can we define it? For the purpose of this book, organizational agility is defined as a set of managerial and organizational capabilities that allow the organization to adapt quickly under conditions of fast-paced change. We will return to this definition and its implications for organizational structures in the future in Chapter 5.

Analysis of the determinants of agility provides insights into those aspects or dimensions that characterize the agile firm. The literature on firm agility points to several individual- and organization-level determinants of agility.

Dove (1995) focuses on the importance of agile resource management at the individual (or manager) level. It is the management that will be able to guide the organization to proficiency and agility. A company, argues Dove, needs proactive and reactive competences to respond to external events and progressive and resilient capabilities to launch internal change events. Agile firms have managers who proactively demonstrate the ability to anticipate and react to external changes that can affect the company.

Goldman et al. (1995) and Shafer (1999) consider that in an agile company it is the management that cultivates an entrepreneurial company culture. It does this by distributing authority, by providing the resources personnel need, by reinforcing a climate of mutual responsibility for joint success and by rewarding innovation. People and information are the differentiators between companies in an agile competitive environment.

Empowerment is also important. However, Shafer (1999) states that agile workers and managers surpass the idea of empowerment. Agile workers can internalize the strategic purpose of the company and use it to drive their behavior. They can read the market, create events and work in virtual teams. Briefly, as Goldman et al. (1995)

explain, an agile workforce is composed of people who are knowledgeable, informed, flexible and empowered. In these "knowledge factories," which Roth (1996) states as a key feature in an agile firm, the role of leaders will also be different. They must constantly work on design and communicate the strategic purpose and vision without stifling debate. Managers in agile firms also foster an entrepreneurial culture that facilitates both innovation and rapid responses to change (Drucker, 1999; Kivenko, 1995). Boundary-spanning organizations that embrace diversity and cosmopolitanism further enhance the innovative capacity of the agile firm and foster its dynamism (Robertson and Wind, 1983; Tushman and Scalan, 1981). The management's primary task in an agile company is to create and maintain an entrepreneurial culture of reciprocal responsibility for the success of the company. Management skills must relate to a sense of urgency and continual personal improvement. This will help to accelerate responsiveness (Kivenko, 1995).

These knowledge factories rely on a knowledge-driven workforce (Goranson, 1999). First, knowledge is key to successfully navigating unpredictable situations. Second, by relying on knowledge as a driver of agility, the firm cultivates an informed and empowered workforce that can make value-increasing decisions quickly.

In sum, a highly changeable, hypercompetitive external environment is the *raison d'être* of agile companies. Essentially, agile companies are agile because agility is one of the best ways firms can confront constant flux.

At the organization level, the basic assumption of the literature on agility is that if an agile company is one that must have the ability to confront and respond to unforeseen changes, the way these companies are organized should certainly be different. Several structural factors and organizational practices can also foster agility and thereby allow firms to face external unpredictability. Agile firms do not rely on one specific kind of organizational structure but rather develop flexible structures that allow them to move quickly from one state to the other in an effort to tackle the problems associated with a hypercompetitive environment. Fewer layers, flatter structures and more communication each help achieve flexible structures (Hatum, 2007; Vinay et al., 1999; Volberda, 1999).

The ways in which agile companies are organized have to allow them to thrive on change and uncertainty. Having a flexible structure helps companies to reconfigure themselves to deal with different types of environments and also to diverse opportunities (Vinay et al., 1999).

Agile companies do not rely on a single structure; there is not a right structure (Campbell, 1998). Agile companies support multiple, concurrent, highly flexible organizational structures. The goal is to be innovative, to have flexible organizational structures that make rapid decisions.

By the same token, Dove (1995) points out some structural features that agile companies should include. He points out the importance of modularity in the agile firm. A modular firm is composed of different units that are capable of interacting with each other but are not integrated. The interaction in an agile organization should be dynamic and nonhierarchical. This is the best way of communicating, negotiating and interacting freely, thus giving room for maneuver for fast decision-making. The different units will respond to objectives rather than methods, and their behavior will include teamwork within the company and partnerships with other companies.

Agile virtual organizations are an integral part of the firm's competencies (Goranson, 1999). We discuss virtuality next.

What Does Being Virtual Mean?

The idea of virtuality generally refers to the importance of collaborating with others to mutual benefit. Cooperation must occur not only internally among the organizational participants but also with competitors, suppliers and customers, as in the case of Threadless (see Figure 1.2), with the firm embracing constant feedback from consumers and allowing consumers to guide strategic decisions (e.g., product design). Cross-functional teams, virtual companies and partnerships even with direct competitors are all means employed to leverage resources through cooperation.

A virtual organization is "an opportunistic alliance of core competencies distributed among a number of distinct operating entities within a single large company or among a group of independent companies" (Goldman et al., 1995: 87).

The virtual organization mechanisms are as follows: partnership, joint venture, strategic alliance, new corporation, cooperative agreement, royalty or license, and outsourcing contract. The characteristic of a virtual organization is the opportunism for rapidly producing and offering a specific product or service (Wildeman, 1998).

Goldman and his associates (1995) and Campbell (1998) introduced the concept of *agile web* or *virtual web*. This is one step forward from the idea of simple collaboration. It is an open-ended collection of prequalified partners who agree to form a pool of potential members of virtual organizations. One of the features of this web or virtual organization is that they create strategy and structure at the same time. The network of relations both guides the action and also provides strategic direction; this idea defies Chandler's (1962) argument that structure follows strategy.

Goranson (1999) also considers an agile company to be a virtual organization. These virtual organizations are opportunistic aggregates of smaller units acting as if they were "large and long-lived" firms. When the opportunity fades, the virtual company fades.

What Does an Agile and Virtual Company Look Like?

Based on the above discussion, an agile and virtual firm is a permeable entity open to receiving information from and sharing information with external sources in an effort to nourish the organization. Such organizations, as the literature highlights, are at their essence innovative. Different types of innovation (such as product or service innovation) will be necessary to adapt quickly in an ever-changing environment (Eisenhardt and Tabrizi, 1995).

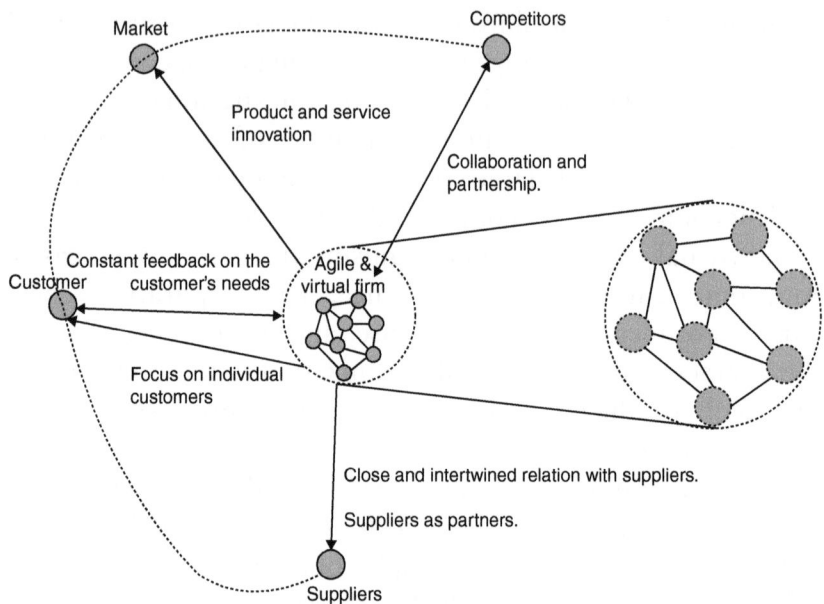

Figure 1.3 *Features of an agile and virtual organization*

Agility and virtuality will both help facilitate the innovative capacity of the firm (Lewin et al., 1999). Such organizations are also early adopters of new strategies, likely to seize the initiative and surprise competitors (Evans, 1991; Webb and Pettigrew, 1999). One might find that agile and virtual firms further apply disruptive strategies that illustrate their weak ties (low embeddedness) with the institutional environment (Anderson and Tushman, 1990; Webb and Pettigrew, 1999). Growth and profitability will be the aim of agile and virtual firms (Goldman et al., 1995).

Figure 1.3 illustrates what an agile and virtual organization looks like, and Table 1.2 summarizes the properties associated with agile and virtual firms.

Agility and virtuality are spreading across firms worldwide. Malone et al. (2003: 10) describe the main differences between the previous ways of organizing and agile, virtual firms as follows:

> [M]assive firms are subject to the organizational innovations of the time: internal disaggregation, partnerships

Table 1.2 *Properties associated with agile and virtual firms*

Properties	Indicators
Proactive management	Proficient managers anticipate and respond to external changes Dynamics and demographics of the dominant coalition Boundary spanning
Knowledgeable workforce	Managers are empowered to make decisions quickly and thereby navigate the firm through unpredictable situations Knowledge-driven organization
Entrepreneurial culture	Emphasis on innovation and rapid response to change
Boundary-spanning organization	Diversity Cosmopolitanism
Flexible structures	Multiple, concurrent, highly flexible organizational structures Horizontal organization Fast responsiveness capacity Low levels of formalization and decentralization of decision-making
Virtual organizations	Collaboration through, for example, partnerships, joint ventures, strategic alliances, outsourcing, web-based resources
Innovative capacity	Product, service, process and organization innovations Early adopters
Adaptiveness capacity	Exploratory and exploitative activities
Strategic agility	Early adopters/fast movers Preemptive maneuvers (seize initiative, surprise competitors) Disruptive strategies Speed and surprise

with members of industry ecosystems or supply chains, reliance on the new venture sector to develop new products or technologies. [. . .] [T]he extreme embodiment of these new organizational principles is the so-called "virtual company," where a small core is linked by technology to a web of partners.

This new type of enterprise presents new challenges for firms in terms of the role of HR, process definition and leadership style. Whether a firm adopts crowdsourcing, open business models or some other new way of organizing, at the end of the day it will have to confront these challenges associated with agility and virtuality. Agile and virtual firms also face the challenge of incorporating a new workforce. Adapting their organizations to accommodate the demographic changes is critical to ensuring that companies succeed in implementing the new ways of organizing.

Our discussion so far has been a general one of the changes organizations will be facing in the near future. In the following chapters, we delve more deeply into the managerial practices and organizational arrangements necessary to incorporate the new generations into the workplace.

Future Trends: A Tale of the Future Workplace[14]

On this spring morning in 2020 there are more people present in the office today than is normally the case. Many workers are here for specialist training from dedicated and highly-qualified training staff. Attendance at the course is not mandatory and it doesn't need to be. Staff are here because they want to be – almost all recognize that they need to develop their skills if they are to maintain their privileged positions and lifestyles. Many are fully aware just how privileged they are – there is a growing group of younger people who have struggled to find work since leaving school. With few qualifications their options are limited. A range of both employer and government retraining schemes have mitigated the problem but youth unemployment is an ongoing political and social issue. This has had the effect of emphasizing the value of education to young people and their parents.

Back in the workplace, monthly metrics are being gathered by what used to be the human resources function. These metrics monitor the productivity of employees by measuring the quality of knowledge and ideas within the organization. Management bonuses are based, in part, on these metrics.

As our office staff return home on that spring-time evening in 2020, they reflect on how their working lives have changed – their active and continuing pursuit of knowledge has been rewarded in an economy that is undersupplied with talent. Consequently, there is also an opportunity for less qualified individuals to "cross the divide" and become knowledge workers. Becoming a member of the elite worker group requires not just knowledge but the desire to gain and develop knowledge.

Compared to ten years ago elite workers enjoy a more supportive management style and have more flexibility to do their jobs in a style that suits them. For the skilled and educated, work has changed and changed for the better.

Ideas at a Glance

The Agile and Virtual Organization

- The agile and virtual firm is comprised of internal networks between different units that have interconnected, synergic and complementary relationships.

- Such firms are open to information exchange and collaboration with external sources, through partnerships, strategic alliances and web-based information-sharing platforms, among other mechanisms.

- Agile and virtual organizations are knowledge-based organizations, where individuals are empowered to make value-added decisions quickly.

- Organizations have to build capabilities to be able to participate in networks. Such participation does not imply total integration, which would reduce the capacity of the organization to innovate.

Questions for Managers

- Is the core value underlying the formal organization of your company becoming an inertial force for adapting, innovating and moving forward?

- The new models of organizing imply high levels of decentralization. Are the benefits of decentralization important for your firm?

  o Is decentralization providing more motivation, creativity, flexibility?

- Do the benefits of decentralization compensate for the potential problems associated with decentralizing?

- Is your workforce prepared to take on the additional autonomy implied by greater decentralization?

- What are the key decisions that should be centralized, and what are the decisions that can be decentralized?

- Are your senior management team and middle managers ready for the challenge of adopting a more agile and virtual way of organizing?

CASE IN POINT: OPEN BUSINESS MODEL AT ELBULLI

From left to write: Ferran Adrià, owner of elBulli restaurant; white sangria in suspension; Montjoi Bay from the restaurant's terrace. Photos courtesy of the company. Credits: Fransec Guillamet.

One of the best examples of an open business model is elBulli, a restaurant owned and operated by Ferran Adrià and Juli Soler since 1990. Located in Rosas, a remote location in Catalonia, Spain, elBulli developed a reputation for so-called *molecular cuisine*, a term that Ferran Adrià qualified as follows: "What we do here is avant-garde cuisine. A radical avant-garde cuisine, which is why our popularity is so strange. Our popularity is not normal!"[15]

Notwithstanding Adrià's disbelief regarding the restaurant's popularity, elBulli received some of the industry's highest accolades. For example, it was a three-star Michelin restaurant, the highest recognition in the industry indicating exceptional cuisine, and it was judged best restaurant in the world four times in a row by *Restaurant Magazine*, another sought-after industry award. elBulli was also popular with the public, receiving over 2 million reservation requests for only 8,000 available reservations during the six months it was open for dinner each year (the rest of the year it is dedicated to elBulliTaller, a research and development space focused on innovation and creativity).[16]

elBulli is a good example of an open business model as described by Sandulli and Chesbrough (2009). Initially, the restaurant's knowledge did not originate inside elBulli but outside. Adrià was involved in the discoveries in molecular gastronomy by Hervé. He also participated in INICON, a European Union project that aims to promote collaboration between scientists, chefs and restaurants. The ideas that Adrià learned through these collaborations were absorbed by and even improved upon at elBulli. Such was the interest in Adrià's creations that the School of Engineering and Applied Sciences at Harvard appointed him professor for one of its courses. As Adrià notes, "[elBulli is] offering a science course at Harvard. This will make all universities in the world wonder how come Harvard got interested in cooking and has made a serious thing about it. Cooking is a universal activity, and this will be an interesting phenomenon that will bear consequences."[17]

In addition to drawing knowledge from outside the company, elBulli shared the knowledge that it acquired with a number of other businesses. For instance, elBulli's success allowed partners Juli Soler and Ferran Adrià to invest in elBulli Carmen, which manages ventures related to catering, hotels and new technology, and in elBullibooks, elBulli's publishing house. elBulli also shared its knowledge with elBulli Hotel, which serves dishes from seasons past. Other forms of knowledge sharing that the company engaged in include co-branding ventures with Borges aromatic oils, Italian coffee company Lavazza and Lays (PepsiCo), and a collaborative alliance with NH hotels to develop NHube, a new restaurant concept, and Fast Good, a project that aims to prove that eating fast and healthy is possible. The company also shared knowledge by publishing a general catalog annually starting in 2002. These catalogs provided a retrospective and an evolutionary map of the company's work and innovations, where organization, philosophy, products, technology, process and styles all become interrelated. "Do you know why we do it?" asks Adrià. "Because this year's elaborations are history. Sure, this means pushing the creativity boundaries . . . but that is our adrenalin."[18] "To open yourself up and teach," adds Oriol Castro, "that is what makes you big."[19]

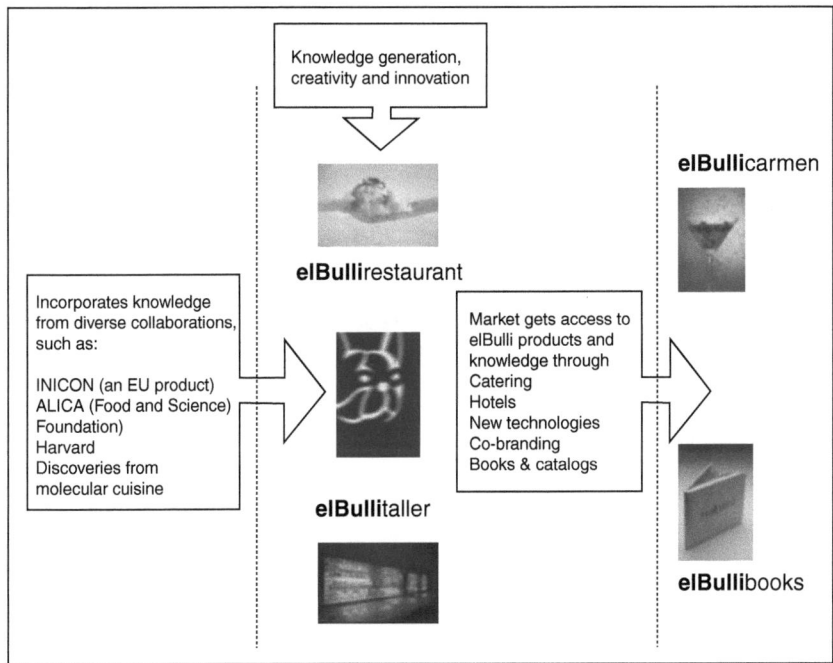

Figure 1.4 *Open business model at elBulli*

The restaurant has recently closed its doors. Why, if elBulli was so successful and famous, would Adrià decide to close it? "elBulli will not end, it will transform," explains Adrià. "It will re-open in 2014 as elBulliFoundation, a foundation that aims to train people in gastronomic creativity and innovation."[20] Figure 1.4 shows the dimensions that characterized the open business model at elBulli.

As the discussion above illustrates, elBulli's knowledge sharing reflected both the buyer's and the seller's perspective of the open business model – the company engaged in collaborations and partnerships with other organizations to learn and thereby expand its knowledge, and at the same time the company participated in ventures with other firms and organizations to share its knowledge and thereby increase the firm's impact.

The fact that the restaurant will be closed for two years while Adrià and his team develop the new foundation (which will include the restaurant) is far from a departure from the open business model that has characterized the restaurant. Indeed, in a recent interview Ferran Adrià was clear about the aims of the new venture:

> At the new elBulli, it will be critical to share everything we do. This is our essence. Everything that will be created will be shared everyday by internet. In 2014 you will get access to a file and get all our research and creative experience. This has got a social impact, why not share creativity? This was and will be our best way to collaborate with society.[21]

2
Demographic Changes in the Workplace

DIFFERENT GENERATIONS AND PERSPECTIVES

While new ways of organizing will be increasingly important for firms to succeed in the future, the deep demographic changes occurring in the workplace will also be important to take into account. Indeed, firms are already facing the challenge of transforming their structures and ways of organizing to incorporate the new generation.

Never before have organizations seen three and even four generations working together. These overlapping generations have great implications not only for the way work is performed but also for the way firms need to think about their future talent management strategies and the HR practices required to support their human capital. Heterogeneity and diversity have replaced the homogeneous workforce that pervaded before.

Much has been written about the different generations in today's workplace and about the Millennials in particular. Here, the aim is not to simply reiterate previous studies. The previous chapter analyzed changes in the way firms organize. This chapter connects the demographic changes with the organizational ones to shed light on the correlation between these changes and the difficult task companies face when thinking about attracting, developing and retaining talent.

The generations working together today that are relevant for the purpose of this study are as follows: baby boomers,

Generation X (Gen X) and Generation Y (Gen Y), or the so-called "Millennials." Baby boomers refers to the postwar generation, born between 1946 and 1964; Generation X refers to individuals born between 1965 and 1980; and Generation Y refers to persons born between 1981 and 1997 (Guthridge et al., 2008; Terjesen and Frey, 2008). We will only briefly refer to Generation Z (Gen Z) or Generation 2020 (Meister and Willyerd, 2010), which comprises those people born after 1997 and still not in the labor market. The so-called "traditionalists," born between 1900 and 1945, are also mentioned only briefly due to the fact that very few of them are still working today.

Meister and Willyerd (2010) point out that the number of US workers over the age of 40 has increased significantly. By 2010, 51% of the US workforce was 40 years of age or older, while Millennials represented only 22% of the workforce. However, by 2014 Millennials are expected to make up almost 47% of the US workforce. These figures suggest that an impressive replacement of the workforce will occur over a relatively short period of time and thus underscore the emphasis companies will have to place on adapting to the fast-changing demographics.

Besides these demographic changes, many of the new jobs created since the beginning of the 1990s have focused on the knowledge economy (Johnson et al., 2005). These jobs require a complex set of skills related more to intellectual capabilities (i.e., analysis, decision-making etc.) than technical skills.

What Are the Main Features of the Different Generations?

Traditionalists served their countries during the Second World War. But they also witnessed the First World War and participated in the Korean War. Loyalty, respect and honor define the values of the traditionalists. Many of them have military experience and as a result the managerial style of this generation tends to follow a top-down approach to getting things done.

Not surprisingly, traditionalists embrace the idea of working with large institutions, as they view such institutions as the source of a stable career that one can be proud of.

Baby boomers are still a large workforce. However, as of 2012, baby boomers were between their 40s and retirement age. The fact that a large proportion of the current workforce is near retirement is a huge challenge for firms that need to build a bridge between generations to prepare for their continued success in the future.

Baby boomers witnessed the Cold War, the Vietnam War, Watergate, the first time a man walked on the moon as well as the civil rights struggle and the assassination of President Kennedy. Moreover, they were able to watch each of these events on TV. Indeed, one could say this generation was raised with the TV. Power was being shared by two generations, baby boomers and traditionalists. Boomers were raised under a top-down managerial approach but needed to learn how to build consensus. This is an optimistic generation that has been able to live in a wealthy and rich world.

After the baby boom generation, babies went bust, with the birthrate declining dramatically. This new smaller generation, Gen X, accounts for managers in their mid-30s through mid-40s. This generation has witnessed great technological developments and is technologically savvy, though Gen Xers are digital immigrants. The toppling of the Berlin Wall, the AIDS epidemic, the drug crisis and the Persian Gulf War were among the most important events this generation witnessed in its formative years. The skeptical Gen Xer has seen many parents divorce, corporate scandals, corruption and well-established institutions be called into question.

While boomers' lives were impacted largely by the TV (Tapscott, 2009), many inventions have changed Gen Xers' lives and way of work: cable TV, fax machines, video games, Palm Pilots, pagers, mobile phones and personal computers, among others. Not surprisingly, Gen X has clashed with the other generations still in the workplace. As Lancaster and Stillman (2010) put it, the managerial style of the three generations can be described as "chain of command" (traditionalists), "change of command" (baby boomers) and "self-command" (Gen X). Given these different management styles, such clashes have been in a sense predictable. See Table 2.1 and 2.2 for understanding the main features and events throughout different generations analysed and their differences.

The Unresolved Challenge: The Silver Tsunami

"In 1950, there were seven working age people for every elderly person in the United States. By 2030, there will be only three ... Since 1950, the number of people aged 65 and older in the United States has increased from 8% to 12%. According to the U.S. Census Bureau, the number of people aged 55 and older will increase to 73% by 2020, while the number of younger workers will grow only 5%." These are just some of the figures that Nancy Lockwood (2003) disclosed of the aging workforce in her study, which aims to increase awareness of the related challenge organizations will have to confront. The aging workforce has been dubbed the *silver tsunami*.

Countries other than the United States also face an aging workforce. For example, in 2020 Japan will have the same share of its population over the age of 65 as the United States will in 2030 (Lockwood, 2003). And while Americans over the age of 65 will make up more than 16% of the population within 10 years, Germany is aging even faster: More than one-fifth of the country (21.6%) will be over the age of 65 by 2020 (Loch et al., 2010).

One of the factors contributing to the aging workforce worldwide is that people are living longer. This is raising concerns about social detachment and isolation. In the workplace, older workers have a sense of accomplishment and responsibility. Moreover, given the prospect of living

Table 2.1 Main features throughout different generations

	Traditionalists	Baby boomers	Generation X	Millennials
	1900–1946	1946–1964	1964–1979	1980–1997
Main events witnessed	First World War Great Depression New Deal Second World War Korean War	Cold War Vietnam War Watergate First man on the moon Kennedy assassination Civil rights struggle	Berlin Wall taken down AIDS Drugs Gulf War	September 11 Iraq War War in Afghanistan Corporate scandals
Technology evolution	Radio	TV Long plays	Fax Personal computer TV cable Mobile phone VCRs Calculators	Texting Social networks The "I" era (iPod, iPhone, iPad) Internet DVDs/Blue ray

Table 2.2 Inside the different generations: The differences

	Traditionalists	Baby boomers	Generation X	Millennials
Slogan	"We built a legacy"	"What an amazing career we built"	"I have the capabilities I need to succeed"	"We are going to rock the workplace"
Managerial style	Top-down	Top-down Build consensus	Self-control Competition	Not yet fully developed
Values	Loyalty Respect Honor	Competitiveness Hardworking Optimistic	Autonomy Freedom Individualism	Teamwork Flexibility Social awareness
Loyalty	To the firm	To the job	To the profession, to the boss	To the project, colleagues, boss
Feedback	"No news, good news"	Once a year	Frequently	All the time
Rewards	Satisfaction with a job well done	Money Status Job titles	Learning opportunities Work–life balance	A job with sense Growth opportunities Work–life integration

for decades on increasingly reduced retirement funds, graying individuals generally plan to continue working past the traditional retirement age.

Organizations thus have an enormous challenge ahead: They need to balance the need to incorporate new people into the company and train new talent against the fact that their current employees will want to work longer. To meet this challenge, organizations may need to adapt their training and office infrastructure for the aging generation, and older employees will need to be mentally prepared for working into their 60s and even into their 70s. As Dychtwald et al. (2006) point out, however, few large firms are preparing for this transformation of the workforce.

One company that is trying to cope with the aging workforce is BMW. In what the *Harvard Business Review* calls an experiment in "defusing the demographic time bomb" (Loch et al., 2010), BMW has decided to search for ways to plan ahead.

At one of BMW's large auto plants, the average age of employees is expected to rise from 39 to 47 by 2017. Because an aging workforce is associated with reduced productivity, this trend puts the company's future competitiveness at risk. However, at BMW encouraging older workers to retire early or following other traditional ways to reduce the age of the workforce is not desirable. One reason is that older workers have more patience and skill that comes from experience, attributes that are assets on a production line. However, older workers have less flexibility, strength and vision, attributes that are "real liabilities on a production line that depends on precision engineering and a lot of hard work." The question, then, was how should BMW adapt the production process to accommodate an aging workforce?

In a pilot project at the auto plant, the company made 70 small productivity-enhancing changes in the workplace. For example, to reduce the chance of errors as well as physical strain, changes were made to everything from the shoes worn by line employees to the material of the floors they stood on. In addition, some employees were given a place to sit, while tools were improved and new, larger computer screens were introduced. BMW says that, in total, the project cost only about US$50,000, including lost time.[1] The results? Productivity went up 7%. Absenteeism fell below the plant's average, and the assembly line's defect rate dropped to zero.[2]

Notwithstanding the case of BMW, companies by and large are still using an antiquated model for dealing with aging employees. This model assumes that people should get pay rises and promotions on the basis of age and then exit when they reach retirement. Companies have typically dealt with the burdens of this model by periodically "downsizing" older workers or encouraging them to take early retirement.[3] Creativity in the way organizations manage the future of their aging workforce will be critical. The aging workforce will lead organizations to rethink training, office infrastructure and workforce planning.

Ideas at a Glance

Different and Overlapping Generations

- Up to four overlapping generations currently coexist in the workplace:

  1. Traditionalists, born between 1900 and 1945. This generation is characterized by loyalty to the firm, respect and honor.

  2. Baby boomers, born between 1946 and 1964. This generation is competitive, optimistic and hardworking.

3. Gen X, born between 1964 and 1979. This generation values individualism and needs autonomy and freedom.
4. Gen Y or Millennials, born between 1979 and 1997. This generation values work–life integration and a flexible workplace that allows them to multitask and make use of technology.

THE MILLENNIAL GENERATION: "WE ARE GOING TO ROCK THE WORKPLACE"

Many articles and books have attempted to describe Millennials – also referred to as Generation Y, Generation.com (due to their natural ability for handling technology) and Generation Next, among others (Howe and Strauss, 2000) – in an effort to understand their behavior as well as how this new generation fits in the workplace.

Millennials have been variously depicted as self-absorbed, distrustful, unloyal, unconcerned with rules and superficial, among other not particularly flattering adjectives. However, these pessimistic descriptors do not help firms understand how to work with and support these new entrants to the workforce that in America alone will account for 58 million people by 2014 (Sujansky and Ferri-Reed, 2009).

Realistic is the best adjective to describe this new workforce. Consider for a moment where Millennials are coming from: For the most part, they are children of baby boomers who dedicated their lives to companies and ended up having to jump from job to job over the course of their lives and careers. The economic conditions and crises affecting the boomer generation required that they shift jobs and careers. As a result, the Millennial generation did not grow up in an era of increased job security as their parents had but instead in a period of reduced job security and the weakening of ties between employee and employer. Millennials' loyalty thus rests more with themselves and less with the company. For example, if they feel the company is not providing the opportunities they are looking for, Millennials are quick to move on, that is, to quit their jobs and offer their talent to competitors.

We will be analyzing Millennials' characteristics and their impact on the workplace throughout the book. We start here by highlighting four main values that drive their behaviors, attitudes and interests. In particular, this generation values multitasking, the role of technology and being connected, work–life integration and social consciousness. These four values will impact firms' way of organizing in the future.

Figure 2.1 summarizes Millennials' core values and relates them to the concept of the agile and virtual firm.

To elaborate, first, this generation has been noted for its ability to juggle many things at the same time. Younger people have been raised in a context of great stimulation, which has allowed

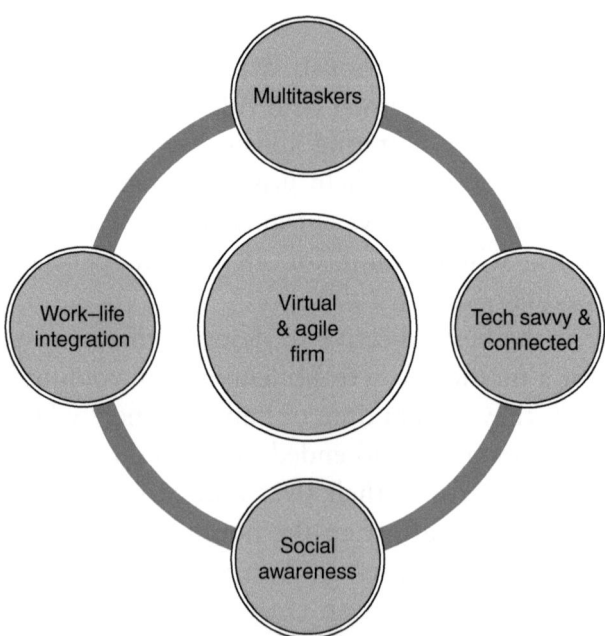

Figure 2.1 *Millennials in the agile and virtual firm*

them to develop strong multitasking skills. This young workforce can perform business tasks while listening to music and interacting on Facebook from time and time. Some managers might consider attention given to nonwork tasks disrespectful. However, this is a common pattern that many Millennials respond to.

Second, for much of their lives Millennials have been connected to the world through texting, internet chats, surfing on the web or social networks. They contact their friends through Facebook and create ideal "selfs" in Second Life. Podcasting and blogging complement the diverse communication forms that this generation embraces.

The Pew Research Center[4] considers the relationship between this generation and technology unique. Social networks are used by this generation to keep up with family and friends and to expand their social network. Indeed, 86% of Generation Nexters (as the study calls Millennials) use the internet, and 51% send and receive text messages on their mobile phone each day. Millennials view Facebook, MySpace and Yearbook as indispensable social networks. All the time they spend on the internet makes Millennials masters of multitasking. They are able to work on many things at the same time, and they expect their jobs to offer and resemble the diverse world they have grown up in with respect to access to technology.

Furthermore, in a survey conducted by Accenture,[5] Millennials indicate that they want to choose which technologies they use rather than be forced to use those supplied by their employer, and they expect to be able to access the applications of their choice. This study suggests that 52% of all Millennials surveyed consider state-of-the-art equipment and technology in the workplace as crucial considerations when selecting an employer.

While this generation is able to multitask and is technologically quite savvy, it is easily distracted. Not surprisingly, companies and schools alike are changing their approach toward capturing the attention of this attention deficient generation. Later in the book, we analyze in detail what firms are doing and what they need to do further.

Third, this generation will pressure organizations to offer work–life integration as well as a real corporate business responsibility strategy that allows the company to make a difference in the community. As the term *work–life integration* suggests, Millennials aim to integrate their work and life, not just to balance their work and life, which might be not enough for them. Their diverse activities (of which work is one) require involving their work, and workplace, in the nonwork aspects of their lives.

Finally, organizations should also respond to the greater importance this generation places on social and environmental problems. Millennials want their work to reflect their personal interests and ethics, and are proud to work for companies that have a positive social or environmental impact.

A good example of a company that tries to allow employees to integrate life and work and at the same time endeavors to have a social impact is Canadian entertainment company Cirque du Soleil. Cirque du Soleil is well known for performances such as Alegría, Varekai, Dralion and Quidam, among its 22 productions touring worldwide or shown at a permanent location. Cirque du Soleil has 5,000 plus employees, of which more than 1,000 are artists. The young artists have a particular ethos and are very demanding not only about their work environment but also about the circus's impact on society.

To foster work–life integration, Cirque du Soleil subscribes to the principle of equal opportunity employment without distinction, exclusion or preference. The company is committed to providing and maintaining a harassment-free climate in the workplace, to guarantee each individual employee's physical and psychological integrity.

In addition, Cirque du Soleil's employee compensation packages include not only salary but also group insurance, a pension plan and paid holidays. Cirque du Soleil also offers indirect benefits such as a subsidized cafeteria, free parking and no dress code requirements. Health and safety are also integrated into the core beliefs of the entire range of the company's operations. Cirque du Soleil further makes a point of supporting cultural discovery and encouraging artistic creativity among its employees in the workplace.[6]

Regarding the social impact of Cirque du Soleil, which is of great importance to its employees, its Global Citizenship initiative is a comprehensive one that involves Cirque in communities and in particular with at-risk youth.[7] One such initiative is Cirque du Monde. The main social program run by Cirque du Soleil, Cirque du Monde uses circus techniques together with educational intervention to help young people at risk. Artists, instructors and coordinators alike are involved in the initiative.[8]

Table 2.3 summarizes some of the possible implications of Millennials' for defining characteristics for both firms' organizational design and individual employees.

Turning to our discussion in the previous chapter on the ways firms organize, Millennials are joining the workforce under the widest scope of organizational forms ever seen in companies – from the simple functional form that is still alive and well in many firms to the boundaryless virtual firm that is expanding the way firms organize (see Figure 2.2). Not surprisingly, Millennials are attracted to models such as crowdsourcing or open business systems. Sujansky and Ferri-Reed (2009) even suggest that Gen Yers are as twice as likely as baby boomers to be "serial entrepreneurs."

With more Millennials entering the workplace, organizations are having to change the way they are organized. Millennials are shaping these changes in a number of ways. Most importantly, the new workforce is encouraging companies to move away from old paradigms of management in favor of new ways of organizing that provide this generation opportunities to develop in a context of freedom and flexibility. The organizational wider scope that companies have to deal with can be easily handled by Millennials. However, integration is a critical issue to make sure that this new generation positively focuses its energy into the organization.

As an example of how companies are integrating Millennials into the workplace, consider the case of Infosys Technologies. Infosys is India's second-largest outsourcing group. Aware of the demographic changes taking place and the importance of social

Table 2.3 *Implications of Millennials' characteristics*

Millennials' characteristics	Organizational implications	Personal implications
Work–life integration	• Allow more flexible schedules • Incorporate work activities in daily lives • Incorporate social networks at work	• Work and life are integrated, not separate and different activities • No need for balance but rather merge both life and work
Multitasking	• Create a more dynamic work environment • Allow participation in multiple activities • Encourage team-building activities, cultural learning opportunities and empowerment • Provide a flatter and networked structure	• Need for variety and different focuses
Tech savvy	• Allow widespread use of technologies • Allow personal choice of technologies • Integrate Gen Y in IT decisions • Incorporate portals and shared workspaces as part of daily job • Take into account career network, home networks and wireless networks	• Emphasis on communication, collaboration and technology
Social awareness	• Corporate social responsibility (CSR) is part of the firm's value proposition • CSR is integrated into Gen Yers' careers	• Greater awareness of social and environmental problems • Social awareness key in job selection

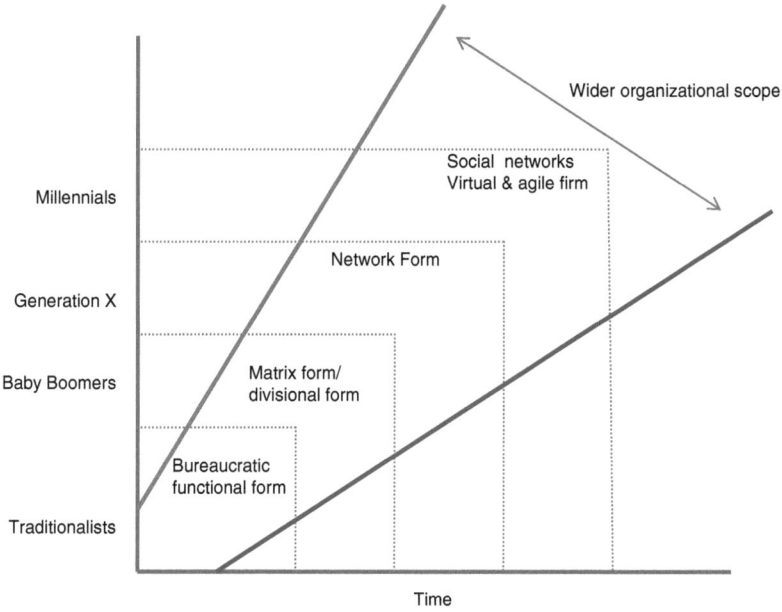

Figure 2.2 *Organizational scope over time and across generations*

networks for Millennials, Infosys has set up its own intra-firm collaboration software, iEngage. This social network, in addition to other forms of internal communication systems, has allowed Infosys to facilitate collaboration and thereby engage the younger workers in their jobs.[9]

More Millennials entering the workplace is also leading to more overlapping generations at work than ever before. Addressing the different management styles and values of the different generations is an issue that firms have to tackle to make sure that workers are successfully integrated into the firm. Some companies are working hard to avoid generational clashes by supporting diverse activities that aim to build intergenerational connections. As Martin and Tulgan (2006) suggest, other generations are interested in learning how Millennials want to be managed, why they feel so entitled and what it is they want at the end of the day.

Of course, one can suggest that workers engage in honest communication and polish their emotional intelligence in an effort to understand others' feelings and needs. But how exactly do these recommendations get incorporated into a company's day-to-day life? Some firms are experimenting with diversity workshops, mentoring and reverse mentoring as ways to connect the different generations. IBM Corp., for example, has developed Mentor Me, which allows employees to use the company's intranet to request a mentor. Employees can seek mentors in a variety of areas, such as general career development or technical skills enhancement, and the system identifies suitable matches from a pool of volunteers. IBM also offers a reverse mentor program for senior executives who wish to learn from recent college graduates how technology is being used by consumers. These exchanges help ease senior employees' fear of passing on power while readying the next generation to lead.[10]

Companies should build bridges between generations in the workplace to ensure the different generations are able to coexist productively. Organizations that fail to deal with diversity in their workplaces will risk facing intergenerational conflict. Organizations must aim at optimizing the talents of all age groups, reconciling differences in the workplace and leveraging this diversity for individual and organizational advantage (McGuire et al., 2007). The case of IBM is one of many in the market that is trying to be open minded and innovative while working with the needs of the different generations.

While Millennials might seem similar as a group, international firms have observed differences worldwide, which create further challenges for those companies with operations in different countries. Many studies have found differences in this generation's behavior across locations. The next section provides a short discussion that should be of particular benefit to multinationals and highlights differences and similarities between Millennials around the world.

ARE GENERATIONS SIMILAR WORLDWIDE? INDIA, CHINA AND THE WEST

Can we talk about Millennials as a homogenous group across Europe, America and the BRIC countries? The answer may be no – some differences may need to be acknowledged by firms that have to deal with the new generation entering the workforce in different corners of the planet. First, characteristics of generational groups in western economies, where talent strategies originate, might not address individuals' aspirations in the rest of the world. Second, the generational divisions of the workforce that are commonly used in western countries – such as baby boomers, Gen X and Gen Y – might not well capture the relevant generational divisions in the rest of the world. In line with this view, a *Deloitte Review* study[11] that summarizes the main differences between countries points out that while the concept of three generations (baby boomers, Gen X and Gen Y) starting in 1945 might accurately reflect generational distinctions in the United States, Europe and Japan, it captures such distinctions in other countries less well.

In China, for example, 1949 is a key date, as it corresponds to the founding of the People's Republic. Political turmoil followed, after which came the Cultural Revolution and communism under the rule of Mao Zedong until his death in 1976. The Deloitte study divides the workforce in China by decades. Thus, one will find discussion of the post-1950 generation, the post-1960 generation and so forth. The post-1970 generation (born between 1970 and 1979) is more western in outlook (e.g., first college graduates who chose their own careers and benefited from on-campus recruitment from multinationals, the last generation to be raised on a collective farm etc.). The post-1980 generation, however, is the first generation of single children who are more individualistic, self-centered and disdainful of authority.

In a recent research of managing Millennials in China, Shapero (2012) considers that Millennials are challenging traditional Chinese values. Since its introduction in 1978, the one-child policy has changed the way children are raised in China. With these children known as "the affluent generation" or the "spoiled generation," it is clear that this has had an impact in the way this generation acts. These "little emperors" or "little empresses" are prone to an egocentric, individualistic and materialistic behavior. Shapero states that many of the traditional principles and values of the Chinese society are being challenged by this generation, and this has to be taken into consideration for current and future investors in the country. Some of the assumptions being challenged are the emphasis of correct behavior and image, the emphasis of humility and modesty, the role of authority and the discouragement of initiative.

ASIAM Business Group is specialized in manufacture and quality control processes of textile products in Asia, with its main office in Hangzhou, China.[12] Carlos Montayo, CEO and cofounder of the company, considers that Millennials have been spoilt by parents and grandparents alike. "They are very individualistic and very competitive. They had a huge pressure for being successful."[13]

Moreover, the Chinese Millennials' interest for occidental culture has also shaped this generation:

> They [the Millennials] are very keen on occidental fashion. Their mobiles, clothing brands, their cars, are symbols of status and differentiation. They are extremely ambitious. However, it is very difficult for them to say no, instead you will have answers such as "it will be difficult," "I will do my best." Anyway, all these answers mean no. It is an embarrassment for them to say no. Therefore, it is important to understand what they want to say; they are not very straightforward. They are also very dependent on their parents' decisions for the important things in life, such as your partners, career, even health problems.[14]

With 90% of the workforce being Millennials, the challenges ahead are important for the success of the business:

> When we started operation in China [Moncayo recalls] we tried to hire people with more experience, Gen Xers. However, we soon realized that Chinese Xers have adaptation problems to the way we work. It was difficult for them to understand what empowerment means. They just wanted the boss to make all the decisions. While Chinese Millennials are more adaptable, they also like to change jobs

quickly. They only will stay if they find that their job allows them to be employable in the future; they want to receive constant training and salary increase every 6 months.[15]

In India, in contrast, 1947 is a key date as it marks the end of British rule in the country. Deloitte's study differentiates between three generations specific to India: the traditionalist generation (1948–1968), the nontraditionalist generation (1969–1980) and Gen Y (1981 onward). The traditionalists are characterized as aspiring to lifetime employment and giving back high levels of loyalty in return. The nontraditionalists, who were shaped by the initial experiments in outsourcing, are more entrepreneurial in spirit and favor merit over tenure. Gen Yers in India value development as well as opportunities to work globally.

Deloitte, the audit, tax, consulting and financial advisory firm in more than 150 countries, has two different operations in India with 20,000 employees.[16] The average age of Deloitte's employees is 27 years old, and it represents a big challenge to manage such a young workforce. Nick Van Dam, global director of Learning, e-Learning Solutions & Technologies, considers that attraction in India at the entrance level is easy because there is a huge supply of people who are graduating at university. However, one of the challenges with the Indian workforce is that most of them do not have real work experience: "The education system in India is about knowledge acquisition, but it is not about how to apply the knowledge you have learnt. So we have a first challenge, that is, how to develop people at a faster pace. From an Indian perspective people are very eager to go to the next level. One challenge is how we can provide them with development opportunities and also provide them with new roles so they can be appreciated and recognized."[17] The influence of families on Indian Millennials should be taken into account. "Employment for a person is a family decision, is not an individual decision. So the family is involved in selecting the company, they might join recruitment events, they can also push people for next promotions, or even they can influence their sons' or daughters' decisions of quitting the company and joining another one."[18]

So what is Deloitte doing to incorporate Millennials in their Indian operations?

> We added different levels in hierarchy, so you can be an associate, senior associate, assistant manager, manager, senior manager. In so doing, it allows us to promote people every two years or so. Adding levels and recognition are two leading practices a company has to take into account in India. As an example, in addition to promotion, we recognize people – such as financial recognition. We provide people different opportunities to contribute to the success of the company. They can participate in task force, special project team etc. People expect companies to do a lot from a development perspective. So at Deloitte we have on-boarding programs, managing programs, leadership programs, technology-based learning programs, digital programs for people to grow and develop. Moreover, it is important for them that the company is not just about creating value for the shareholder, but it is also contributing to the society. At Deloitte, India, CSR is important and we ask people to be part of the initiatives we have, and spend time with the social initiatives we have, to work in the communities, education etc. Finally, one of the key things is about using technology. Indians are technology savvy. Social networks are critical for them, to get access to social media. Using the technology for team-building, for connecting people, for recognition is important.[19]

Cross-country generational differences can also be found within the Millennial generation. The Global Workforce Study, conducted by Towers Watson,[20] highlights several differences in attracting and retaining Gen Yers worldwide. For instance, while in Brazil, China and India career advancement and development opportunities are the two most important criteria to attract a candidate to a job, in the United Kingdom and the United States a competitive salary and convenient location lead the ranking in job candidates' preferences.

Previously, it was emphasized the importances of technology to Millennials. However, the importance that Gen Yers place on the availability of technology when choosing an employer may differ across countries. For instance, an Accenture report on Millennials' use of technology[21] suggests that technology features most prominently in Millennials' employer decisions in India (72%), the United States (52%) and China (45%), while it matters less in countries such as Germany (28%), France (26%) and Japan (22%).

To summarize, while Millennials might share some common features worldwide (indeed, they may be more similar across countries than previous generations), some cross-country differences exist that organizations need to take into account when establishing a talent management strategy specific to Millennials. These differences require country-specific policies to succeed in integrating the new generation into the workforce.

Future Trends: The New Cosmopolitans[22]

> There's a new generation of people in the workforce who have been deeply socialized in more than one culture. By deeply socialized I mean that an individual has internalized more than one way of understanding how the world works or another type of help system, where cultures can be thought of as help systems.
>
> We already know that there is a large new demographic where people have incorporated more than one fundamental way of understanding the world. What we are observing is that in the developed economies the top management team is monocultural and is managing an increasingly bicultural or multicultural workforce, whereas in emerging economies the top management tends to be bicultural, or at least has more of a global mind-set, and is managing more monoculturals. India and Mexico are good examples of what we're talking about, where the top management is likely to be bilingual, trained probably in the United States or England.

We can distinguish four major types of biculturals. One type is what I call a "one-home" bicultural, whose self-perception is that they are bicultural but who feel more part of one culture than the other culture. Take, for example, Korean Americans who identify themselves as Korean American and whose parents are from Korea and speak Korean, but who themselves don't speak Korean and feel they are American more than part of their parents' cultural origin. Another example may be African Americans who want to be more African than they are, so they choose to celebrate Kwanzaa or African rituals though they really don't know much about Africa.

The second type of bicultural is what I call a "both and" bicultural. "Both ands" consist of biculturals who are integrated. Consider, for example, US Japanese who know about both the United States and Japan, are bilingual, fluently apply their understanding of the United States and Japan and have developed a sense of themselves that is "both and."

Next there is what I call "neither nor" biculturals. A "neither nor" is a bicultural who is not accepted by either culture.

The fourth type of bicultural is what I call an "either or" bicultural. I think that there are several types of "either ors." In the simplest case, the "either ors" are individuals who, if they are in a US setting, become American, whereas if they are in a Chinese setting, they become Chinese.

Regarding the young generation, the Millennials, it would be interesting to know what percentage of them are deeply socialized in more than one culture and what percentage of them are what I would call the "global cosmopolitans" because I think that this generation has a lot of information about the world available to them through computers and other forms of communication, and thus I would imagine that many feel a certain confidence cross-culturally. They may even have had pen pals. My guess

> is that these "global cosmopolitans" have had a superficial introduction to other cultures but do not have a deep understanding of them, so may in face have a false sense of global understanding.

Ideas at a Glance

The Millennials

- Millennials are masters at multitasking. They are able to work on many things at the same time, and they expect their jobs to resemble the diverse world they have grown up in and to offer wide access to technology.
- Millennials aim to integrate work and life, not just balance life and work.
- Millennials have greater concern for social and environmental problems.
- Millennials emphasize the importance of communication, collaboration and technology.
- Millennials face organizational structures never seen before. Social networks, agility and virtuality are shaping the companies in which Gen Yers are working.

Questions for Managers

- Are overlapping generations considered a problem in your organization?
- Have you analyzed the characteristics and interests of the different generations in your firm?
    - What tools and methodologies have you tried to implement?

- What is your firm doing to make sure Millennials can be integrated into the workplace along with the other generations at your company?

- If you are part of an international firm or corporation, has your company devised general talent management strategies as well as country-specific talent management strategies that aim to understand the local-level aspirations of the workforce?

CASE IN POINT: FRISSE BLIKKEN (FRESH FORCES), NEW ORGANIZATIONAL PARADIGMS FOR NEW TALENT

FRISSE◉BLIKKEN

In the outskirts of Utrecht, the Netherlands, is Frisse Blikken,[23] a company created with a twofold purpose: boost the entrepreneurial spirit of young professionals and support companies that face new challenges with the capabilities, ideas and skills of young professionals. The first time I heard about this small firm, it was difficult for the person introducing the company to explain clearly where the business was and what they were doing.

The facilities in Utrecht are also difficult to explain. While this is not Google with its fancy amenities such as PlayStations and Xboxes, this company can be described as a big open space. Located in a field previously occupied by a technical school, the huge space amazes the visitor. The setting invites people to flock in when they feel they need the space to work. Whiteboards, chairs, computers and coffee are the "tools" employees have at their disposal to create and conduct their work. Simple, yes, but effective.

Fritz Korten is the founder and visionary behind this venture.

> In Holland, our demographic pyramid is degraying at the top and degreening at the bottom, so a lot of people

are leaving the labor force and less young people are entering ... So it is very difficult for organizations to get talent, to find talent and to keep them. At the same time, a lot of organizations face new challenges like the use of social media, the introduction of flexi-working and recruitment by serious gaming – all challenges from which they can benefit from the ideas and fresh minds of the new generation of professionals.[24]

With this idea in mind, Korten and his two partners created Frisse Blikken, a Dutch term that translates to "Fresh Forces."
The most important reason behind the decision to create Fresh Forces is the huge gap between the percentage of students wanting to start a company and that of those who actually are successful in doing so.

Our research showed that 83% of Dutch students want to start a company at some point in their career. On the other hand, only 1% actually start a company during, or in the first three years after, his or her studies. That's very low, and we thought: why, isn't it a pity to postpone entrepreneurship while you're young, energetic and full of ideas? My two partners and I decided that we wanted to build an organization that accelerates and supports young professionals in their entrepreneurship.

Fresh Forces aims to prepare future entrepreneurs and at the same time link them with projects in large companies that seek a fresh approach to problem-solving and innovation.

We offer young talent, after a tough selection process, a full-time job for up to three years. After three years they have to leave our company. We train young professionals to become entrepreneurs; we coach them and help them develop knowledge and marketable skills. How do we do that? Intensive coaching on their projects, internal training, but most of all by giving them freedom, faith and responsibility. We pay them well, with additional incentives according to performance. So these young professionals set their own working hours, holidays and career path. Our mission is to accelerate and deploy young entrepreneurship.[25]

While Korten's description of Fresh Forces may bring to mind the goals of an NGO, unlike a typical NGO this venture earns good profits through contracts with large firms. So companies aiming to tap the knowledge and skills particular to the new workforce, to improve their recruiting systems, or to update and optimize their IT systems are turning to and benefiting from the services of Korten's company. "We hire young professionals, train them and introduce them to big corporations in which they can perform many jobs as if they were project managers. Conducting benchmark studies and improving the searchability and usability of websites are among many of the projects our young professionals are working on."[26]

Photos of the workspace at Frisse Blikken. Courtesy of the company.

Not all applicants are offered an opportunity to work at Fresh Forces, but those who are offered a position with the company receive a number of benefits and experiences that help these young professionals prepare themselves for the future: access to coaching and mentoring by experienced entrepreneurs, experience working with a team on projects in large organizations, experience with entrepreneurial employment (e.g., a three-year contract) and being part of an expensive skills development program, among others. Most importantly, employees at Fresh Forces control the direction of their own careers. Whether a particular young professional would like to become an entrepreneur or a manager for a while is up to him or her. However, as Korten states, one thing is certain: "He or she will have grown as a professional and enterprising person over time."[27]

Agility and virtuality are key to Fresh Forces' success. The way Fresh Forces has structured the company is through cells. Cells are formed by topic on the basis of what the market is requesting of the company. Each cell consists of a team, where the team works on different issues for different firms. "In the age of virtual, you need to move faster. Young professionals like to do that; this is attractive for them and a motivator."[28]

When a young professional comes up with a new idea for a new venture, he or she can become a partner of Frisse Blikken. If the idea is good for the company, a new cell will emerge in which shares are split between the company and the entrepreneur. Everybody wins – the new venture receives initial financial support without which it would be difficult for the new venture to emerge, the new generation's entrepreneurial spirit is supported through mentoring opportunities and compensation for their contributions, Fresh Forces' clients receive expanded access to services and Fresh Forces earns further revenues.

Fresh Forces shows us the importance of both maintaining an adaptable, flexible structure and integrating the new workforce into a dynamic context. Fresh Forces was founded and began operating on April 1, 2011. As of March 1, 2012, the firm counts 17 professionals, is profitable and has a client base that includes almost all of the larger Dutch companies. Most importantly, the atmosphere is energetic, professional and fun.

This page intentionally left blank

3
Attracting Millennials to the Workplace

BUILDING THE EMPLOYEE VALUE PROPOSITION (EVP) TO ATTRACT MILLENNIALS

Having a well-respected, strong brand was once considered critical to be able to attract top talent. It was enough to be a multinational corporation and become highly admired company. The rankings prepared by *Fortune* magazine reflect that perspective. In response to the question "Which firms have the best reputation?" the answer would be "Look at the *Fortune* magazine rankings." Accordingly, for years these rankings have helped elevate companies' prestige. However, is that still enough? Is a good reputation and strong brand sufficient to attract the new generation to one's company?

Young employees who in previous years would have felt obliged to have good reasons to leave employment at a large, stable corporation now expect employers to provide them a compelling reason to stay. In the "decade of the employee," as Jamrog (2002) refers to it, or the "employees' golden era," as Hatum (2010) calls it, an EVP is increasingly important to be able to communicate, attract and retain top talent among today's young workforce. The director of International Recruitment at L'Oréal agrees:

> As a prerequisite to anybody who works in human resources, especially in competitive environments, we need to work

on our employer proposition. Both to see if it sells outside, so that we can attract and recruit the best talent, and also to see whether we can provide the environment where this talent will blossom and develop at the pace we want them to develop.[1]

Theories related to branding and EVP all underscore the importance of an EVP to improve attractiveness, generate greater employee commitment and become the employer of choice (Manpower, 2009). Lancaster and Stillman (2010), however, highlight the importance of "meaning" in referring to the value proposition a company is offering to the younger generation. Thus, it seems that while a strong brand is no longer enough to attract and retain the new generation, the traditional approach to EVP may also be inadequate.

Hatum (2010: 38) defines an EVP as "the firm's organizational features that allow it to promote itself outwardly and generate loyalty internally." Those organizational features are the firm's organizational culture, people, work characteristics and rewards. While the brand provides a message for attracting prospective employees, the EVP delivers the actions and behaviors that are attractive to the target candidates as well as to those already working in the organization. Similarly, Black (2007)[2] argues that value propositions address leadership, company, job and rewards, four areas that are critical to attracting and retaining good people.

It seems, therefore, that a comprehensive EVP needs to address a broad range of elements that are important to employees. A recent study by Towers Watson (2010) points out that when companies formalize their EVP, the EVP is more likely to become a unifying experience.[3] While this is true, both the company's brand and EVP should provide a detailed understanding of critical workforce segments in the organization. And this is where things become more challenging when thinking about Gen Yers entering the force.

The importance of the EVP to enhancing a company's ability to attract the young market of Gen Yers was pointed out earlier.

More and more, attractive employers do not depend on their corporate brand but rather on a sum of intangible attributes that are behind the brand and in line with the EVP. A good idea of the changes going on in the current and future employment market as a result of the entrance of the new generation of employees can be obtained by turning to the Universum rankings, which are based on "the preferences of over 160,000 career seekers, with a business or engineering background from the world's 12 largest economies."[4] Take, for example, the 2011 ranking of global top 50 business employers for career seekers. This global talent attraction index indicates which companies are most attractive to potential young employees. While Google managed to lead the list for a fourth year in a row, the big four auditing firms are close behind (i.e., PwC, Deloitte, Ernst & Young, and KPMG). In contrast, if we look at the rankings based on surveys of undergraduate students in the United States and the United Kingdom, we see that the banking and investment, management consulting and oil and gas industries are perceived as less attractive to young prospective employees.

The most recent country-level results as to which companies current undergraduates consider attractive may be surprising. In the United States, for example, the 2012 results show that companies such as Google (1st), Apple (2nd), Walt Disney Company (3rd), Facebook (12th) and the FBI (13th) are highly attractive to the future young workforce. In Canada, the 2012 results show that of the top ten positions two are government organizations (i.e., Government of Canada (3rd) and Canada Revenue Agency (9th)). In Brazil, the 2011 results show that six of the top ten organizations are domestic firms (Petrobras, Vale, Ambev, Banco do Brazil, Itaú Unibanco and Rede Global).

How do undergraduates' favorite McKinsey and Boston Consulting Group (BCG) rank? Neither ranks high among the largest economies surveyed. In the United States (2012), for example, McKinsey ranks 42nd and BCG ranks 37th,[5] while in Canada (2012) these firms no longer rank among the top 100 firms at all. In France (2012), students from *Grandes Écoles* indicate a preference to work for Coca-Cola (10th) over McKinsey (11th) and BCG (12th).[6] Similarly, in the United Kingdom (2011) retailers John Lewis (14th) and Marks & Spencer (23rd) rank higher than McKinsey (35th) and BCG (51st).[7] Thus, it appears the traditional favorites have lost their flair in the eyes of the young future workforce. According to a study done by Pricewaterhouse-Coopers, the top three sectors in which Millennials do not wish to work solely because of their image are oil and gas, defense and insurance.[8]

In emerging economies in Asia, things are difficult for multinational firms. Talent in emerging economies is scarce and expensive. In China, for example, barely 2 million local managers have English-language skills that multinationals need. McKinsey survey in China found that senior managers in global organizations switch companies at a rate of 30% to 40% a year – five times the global average. Fast-moving and ambitious local firms are competing more strongly. In 2006, the top ten ideal employers in China included only two locals. By 2010, seven of the top ten were Chinese companies.[9]

The difference between the preferences of yesterday's and today's young workforce is even greater if we look at *Fortune* magazine's rankings related to companies' perceived reputation. *Fortune*'s 2011 ranking lists Apple, Google, Berkshire Hathaway, Southwest Airlines, P&G, Coca-Cola, Amazon and FedEx among the top ten firms.[10]

The common features of companies viewed as most desirable to work with are that, in addition to enjoying market success, they offer prospective employees learning opportunities, an environment that will allow them to flourish as well as products or services that are viewed as "cool" and that as a result motivate the young workers. In this context, it is not surprising after all that after the huge financial crisis of 2008–2010 students are punishing financial institutions in their employment choices.

So what can organizations learn from these rankings about the values and motivation of the new generation entering the workforce? How can firms build a better EVP and thereby consolidate their brand in the labor market? What are the new aspects of an EVP that a firm will need to take into account to succeed in attracting and retaining the new young generation into its organization?

Social impact. Millennials are known for their interest in jobs that allow them to make a difference in the world by working on community service projects or projects that support sustainability. This explains why many public organizations are topping the young workforce's preference rankings. By joining a public service organization or a government agency, young people hope to make a real difference in society. In the importance this generation attaches to the environment and sustainability concerns, we can find an answer to the question of why oil and gas firms are not listed among the ideal organizations to work with. The green feeling is strong in Gen Yers and is expected to be even stronger in future generations. A recent survey[11] states that corporate responsibility is critical for Millennials. Of the Millennials surveyed, 88% said they will choose employers who have CSR values that reflect their own, and 86% would consider leaving an employer if CSR values no longer matched their expectations.

The AES Corporation is a global power company with generation and distribution businesses. Through their diverse portfolio of thermal and renewable fuel sources, the company provides energy in 28 countries and accounts for a workforce of 29,000 people worldwide.[12] The company is in a critical sector sometimes not very attractive to Gen Yers. As Kay Penney, regional HR manager for Europe and Commonwealth of Independent States (CIS) countries, commented, "AES is a fossil fuel–based organization; we have a growing renewable business, but our sector is in the full front of the global debate about global warming and energy requirements, among others."[13]

Besides challenges related to the environment, Julian Nebreda, senior regional vice president of AES, identifies other challenges: "We do not have branding, nobody cares who produces energy. Besides, while renewable energy is fun for young people, fossil fuel energy might not be attractive for them."[14] "Every year," continues Kay Penney,

> the bar goes up in terms of making the atmosphere cleaner and cleaner. My sense is that people who work in the wind section in particular, and solar to some extent, are passionate green activists. They really believe it's here – it's real passion to promote wind as a source of energy or renewables as a source of energy. If you then have a career progression conversation in which you say "Good news, I have a gas-fired power station over here for you to go and work in for the next five years," it's not taken to be good news. They like what they are passionate about.[15]

However, things vary within a corporation depending on the market and the context in which the firm is operating. While in Europe energy is today considered a basic right (British Gas started providing gas lighting in 1812), many communities in less developed countries still lack power. Ginette Martin, regional HR manager for Latin America and Africa notes,

> [O]ur plans for Ecuador and Colombia are very successful in those places where we generate awareness of the adequate use of energy. This is not only important for people in the towns we serve but also for employees and the young generation of prospective employees who are attracted when companies are socially responsible.[16]

Teach for America[17] is a good example of an organization that has been rising in the preferences of young students in America. Teach for America is a national corps of outstanding recent college graduates with diverse academic backgrounds and career interests who commit to teach in urban and rural public schools for two years and become leaders in the effort to expand educational opportunities and help solve educational inequity. The 2012 corps comprises more than 4,500 recent college graduates, graduate students and professionals from all 50 states, representing over 500 colleges and universities. Valuing the leadership skills acquired over two years' service with Teach for America, top employers across the United States have started to recruit individuals who have worked with the NGO. Thus, Teach for America has become an elite brand that can help young professionals build their resume, regardless of whether the individual wishes to pursue a career in education. In fact, in 2011, the organization was named one of *Fortune* magazine's 100 Best Companies to Work For.[18] One of the corps referred to the experience of being accepted as akin to "being accepted to an Ivy League grad school."[19]

A third example of a firm focusing on its social impact is software firm Salesforce.com. This firm employs what it refers to as a 1/1/1 model. What does this mean?

a. One percent of time. Employees are offered opportunities to find meaningful ways to spend up to six paid days off a year to devote to volunteerism.

b. One percent of product. CRM[20] licenses are donated or offered at discounted rates to nonprofits to help them increase their data management and operational effectiveness capabilities.

c. One percent of equity. Founding stock is provided to fund grants and to support youth, technology and employee-inspired volunteer projects through monetary assistance.[21]

The 1/1/1 model has boosted the attractiveness of the firm in the young labor market. As the CEO of the company points out, "This program has dramatically increased our ability to recruit and retain high-quality employees."[22]

A window to the world. One employer after another will say this new group of employees is also more globally minded than any before it, and opportunities abroad strike a chord. Consistent with this view, most of the firms or organizations that rank highly in the Universum index either have a global presence or provide opportunities to learn a different culture or language.

A recent report analyzing talent mobility[23] considers that Millennials will make up the significant majority of all international assignments by 2020. They will increasingly view the organization – and the world – without boundaries. They will happily begin their careers outside their home countries if the employment or role prospects are greater abroad. A significant majority of the Millennials we surveyed – 80% – want to work abroad, with 70% expecting to use nonnative languages in their careers and 94% stating they believe they will work across geographic borders more than their parents did. They will continue to follow well-paid opportunities internationally while spending spells in their home countries, but they are just as likely to shift across functional areas, roles, multiple cultures and economies, without the need to return to their home country until perhaps later in their careers. Their focus is on interest and opportunity, not necessarily on monetary rewards, and we foresee for them a fundamental change in the assignment duration, package type and value.

At L'Oréal, for instance, the importance of offering international opportunities to their employees is part of the EVP. In Europe, the company has created a program called Euro Opportunity, where the best talent in one country can pursue internships in a different country. As the director of International Recruitment explains,

> Being a global firm and playing global on careers is something that appeals a lot. So for people who want to be global, they will work on global business development, but also they can have a global career. It is a level more of ambition and people can grow quickly, if they have the desire to go find a career, to stretch and develop themselves.[24]

The Peace Corps[25] is another good example of an organization that offers employees opportunities to get involved in projects around the world while working for a good cause. The Peace Corps traces its roots and mission to 1960, when then Senator John F. Kennedy challenged students at the University of Michigan to serve their country in the cause of peace by living and working in developing countries. From that inspiration emerged an agency of the federal government devoted to world peace and friendship. Since that time, more than 200,000 Peace Corps volunteers have served in 139 host countries to work on projects ranging from AIDS education to information technology deployment and environmental preservation.

Offering an international career experience is important not only for the young workforce in developed countries but also for those in less developed countries. Tonatiuh Barradas, vice president of strategic industries for Latin America at SAP, the world leader in enterprise applications in terms of software and software-related service revenue,[26] commented,

> [O]ne of our main challenges ... in capturing the attention of Gen Yers who, different from earlier generations that worked at only one company over the course of their career, have a vocation and will develop their own ventures is that they prefer to focus on innovation and creativity.[27]

With this in mind, SAP started working on a strategy to attract and retain Gen Yers. In 2011, the company launched a new program for young professionals that offers the possibility of "getting international and regional experience, traveling in Latin America, and getting in touch with experienced managers."[28] This initiative is now being implemented in Argentina, Brazil and Mexico.

The "me brand." Companies that provide good training and development, good references as one advances in his or her career and good leaders who support one's professional development have been favored by young talent worldwide. This includes firms that have been investing heavily in technology to facilitate the development of their workforce worldwide – such as the Big 4 (i.e., Deloitte, KPMG, Accenture and PricewaterhouseCoopers). The biggest draw for Millennials, according to a recent study, is the opportunities of career progression.[29] Fifty-two percent said that they felt that this made an employer an attractive prospect. When asked which factor influenced their decision to accept their current jobs, 65% answered the opportunity for personal development.

At Deloitte, which hosts a global learning platform that provides its entire workforce around the world the opportunity to access technology-based learning solutions, the idea of using education and professional development to support employees' personal brand is clear. According to Nick Van Dam, global director of learning for Deloitte and director of human capital for Deloitte Consulting, "When people consider an employer, one thing they look for is a place where they can take their set of skills to the next level, a place where they can develop, explore their talents and grow their careers."[30] This means that organizations need to build a learning environment, a place where people can reach the next stage of their career, helping them to build their own brand in the labor market.

Such is the importance that Deloitte gives to continued learning that they have started providing professional development opportunities to executives outside the firm. Through Deloitte's Leadership Academy, the firm offers professional development opportunities to executives worldwide based on Deloitte's high standards, expertize and up-to-date technology. See main features of Deloitte's Leadership academy in Figure 3.1.

The German media giant Bertelsmann tries to develop top managers through specialized training programs. In India, for example, its high-potential employees can apply for an INSEAD program. This possibility increases their motivation and brings local market employees to the corporate center, where they gain exposure to the range of functional and geographical issues they can expect to encounter as leaders.[31]

Historically, globally recognized firms have enjoyed significant advantages: They knew they were more attractive to local employees than many local competitors. But today many fast-growing firms have more pulling power to help people build the "me brand." One challenge for global firms is to manage the tension between being globally consistent and, at the same

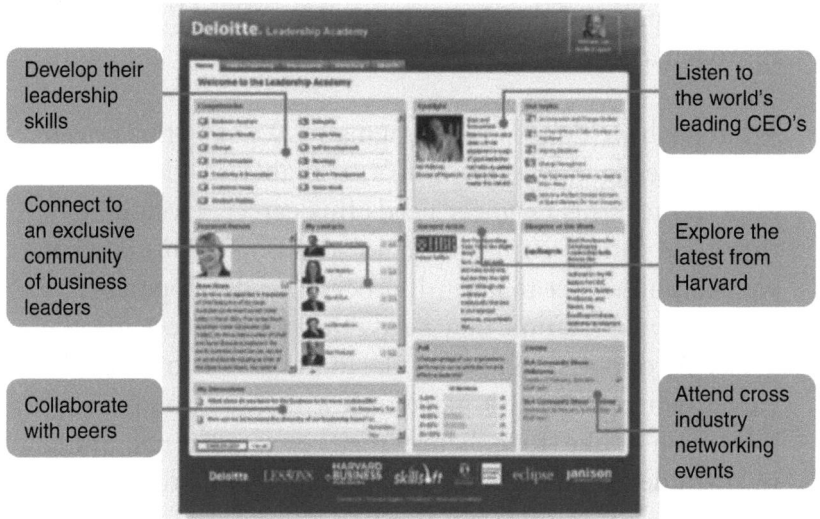

Figure 3.1 *Deloitte's Leadership Academy*
Copyright: Deloitte Development LLC. Author: Nick Van Dam. Used with permission.

time, responsive to very diverse local needs. Tata,[32] the Indian group with a 100 operating companies in seven business sectors, has tailored EVP for each of its major markets; for example, it stresses the quality of its managers to the rest of the employees in India, development opportunities in China and interesting jobs in the United States.[33]

In a recent study on why people are dissatisfied with their current jobs, the main reason that stands out is the lack of opportunities for growth and career advancement.[34] The chief leadership officer at Accenture, states,

> Today's professionals are not job hunting, despite expressing dissatisfaction. Instead, they are focused on their skill sets and on seeking the training, the resources and the people that can help them achieve their goals. Leading companies should support these efforts by listening to employees and providing them with innovative training, leadership development and clearly-defined career paths.[35]

To boost employees' development and growth, AES implements an approach aimed at supporting the "me brand."

> What we have done is very pragmatic. We say "this power station needs this skill, who's available to do it?" as opposed to "this engineer needs this career development, this is his formal path to a senior position." This is what we call pull rather than push process for development. So it's the power station that needs the skills, where are the skills? As opposed to this, it's the individual who needs the career, where's the best place to learn? In so doing, those who would like to enhance their own personal brand through development have a great opportunity to do so.[36]

While learning and development are important, career transitions are also critical to this young generation. At Deloitte, two-thirds of employees who recently left the company did so to do something they could have done within the firm if the firm had made such a transition possible. The company therefore decided to create a position in charge of recruiting and retaining Gen Y, a director of next-generation initiatives. This director is responsible for creating programs at Deloitte that focus on helping people figure out their next career move.[37]

Companies will need to work hard to find the right elements of an EVP that will be a good fit with the characteristics of Millennials that we analyzed in the previous chapter. The EVP has to be thought of in terms of those features that will ensure it will be successful, in particular, by taking into consideration the company's culture and ultimate delivery of what is being promised by the EVP. Table 3.1 summarizes the EVP dimensions to attract and retain Gen Yers according to Millennials' characteristics.

Coty, a global beauty products company, provides us a good example of a well-thought EVP that is integrated into the everyday practices of the company. In 2010, the company's sales were US$4 billion, and it accounted for over 8,500 employees worldwide. While the firm is involved in many product categories, such as fragrances, toiletries, color cosmetics and skin care, fragrances account for 62% of sales. The most renowned fragrances in their

Table 3.1 *EVP dimensions supporting Millennials' characteristics*

Millennials' characteristics	EVP dimensions to attract and retain Millennials
Work–life integration	• The social impact of the job plus the "me brand" dimensions of an EVP support the work–life integration that Gen Yers seek. Both dimensions help Millennials build their own identity and integrate their work and life
Multitasking	• The "me brand" plus the "window to the world" dimensions of an EVP are in line with Millennials' multitasking ability. As high achievers, Gen Yers will work hard and efficiently on different items if their professional development and aspirations can be satisfied
Tech savvy	• It is difficult to establish which dimensions of an EVP previously analyzed can best support this generation's tech savvy. That said, the "me brand" dimension can hold implicitly within this idea, depending on the organization's culture and orientation toward this generation
Social awareness	• The social impact dimension of the EVP supports this generation's social awareness. Gen Yers will be attracted to organizations that offer sustainable, meaningful social engagement

portfolio are Balenciaga, Adidas, Calvin Klein, Davidoff and Jennifer Lopez.[38]

Coty has been working on developing and refining its culture over the past ten years, which the company views as fundamental to attracting and retaining people. Not surprisingly, the importance of the firm's culture has been taken into consideration in building its value proposition. Three words that are part of the firm's value proposition and hence are constantly used in the firm, helping it foster the culture it is building, are *faster*, *further* and *freer*. These three words summarize the company's identity, values and operating mode. (See Figure 3.2, EVP at Coty).

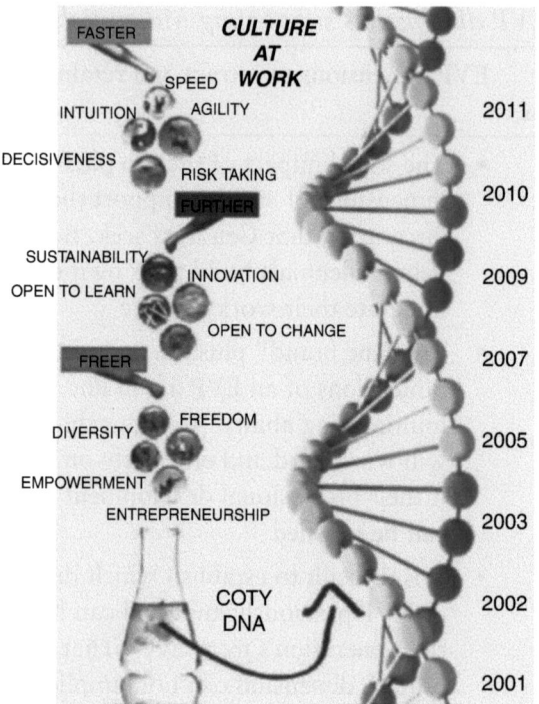

Figure 3.2 *Faster, freer and further: EVP at Coty*
Image courtesy of the company. Used with permission.

"Things change," states Géraud-Marie Lacassagne, head of HR for Coty Group.

> New generations come on board and we need to ask ourselves: Do we still have an appealing proposition, does it still serve the business goals we have? We recently spent nine months having leadership discussions, internal interviews, getting feedback from newcomers, candidates and students . . . . And the conclusion was: yes, more than ever our "faster, further, freer" approach is a strong one that works extremely well for us.[39]

Lacassagne continues, "Everyone dreams of working on our brands – well, not everyone, but more than enough people, compared to the needs of our company. So I'm working more on making sure that we offer the right attractiveness and we build the right EVP according to our culture."⁴⁰

So what does it mean in practice for the company to be *faster*, *further* and *freer*, and how does the company translate these three words into a tight and consistent EVP?

By *freer*, one could believe "I can do whatever I want; I have freedom and if I decide I want to launch a new fragrance line, I can do it." No, this is not what *freer* means. Indeed, we are one organization, we have a clear vision and we have work to do to get there. *Free* means that you are free to invent things, to come up with a novel approach. For example, the fact that everyone works in the same industry is not a reason to do the same thing; people should try things, take risks.⁴¹

Two examples of how the company applies the concept of *freer* in day-to-day operations: Anyone in the organization can talk with the CEO, either via a phone call, e-mail or in his office, if they have an opinion to share or an idea to present. At Coty, *free* also means, "I have the right to disagree with my boss, I have my own opinion, my own belief." In a team meeting at Coty, it is usual to have different opinions raised, with bosses and teams confronting each other in a constructive way. "When we talk, we talk freely, everyone has an opinion, everyone has an idea, everyone can contribute.... However, once a decision is made, all have to align."⁴²

By *faster* the company aims to be very agile, to be able to adapt quickly to changes in a fast-moving market. Agility means empowering employees to make sure they can make good decisions quickly. "Our marketing manager has real empowerment, probably more empowerment at Coty than with some of the other players; he can secure, probably much faster, the necessary approvals and resources for the development of a new product."⁴³

Further in Coty's value proposition refers to being able to anticipate, becoming a leader and not a laggard. Reinventing the rules of the market, the way the firm has to approach the consumer and catch other players by surprise, is included in this idea.

> We came into this industry as a challenger ten years ago. If we had followed rules and accepted the framework already in place, Coty would not today be a leading company in fragrances, the emerging leader in nail care and a fast-growing challenger in color and skin care. One example: ten years ago, everyone in the industry was saying "celebrity perfumes are dead," with only one known sustainable success – Elizabeth Taylor. And then we partnered with Jennifer Lopez. In 2001, we launched her first fragrance "Glow by JLo"; in less than a decade, we have sold over US$1 billion [retail value] with Jennifer alone.[44]

"Faster, further, freer" is not a mere slogan at Coty, but rather is applied in practice. It is very important for companies developing their EVP to make sure their value proposition caters to the values that the new generation is looking to find in companies. Coty shows us how a company brand can be built that suits Millennials: Freedom, fast pace, innovation, creativity and anticipation are desired values for the young people entering the workforce. However, firms have to make sure that organizational fit and strategic alignment are taken into account when thinking about their EVP.

The Unresolved Challenge: The Disengaged Workforce

> The Gallup Organization, a leading international survey research and consulting firm, estimated that "actively disengaged" workers are costing American businesses US$300 billion a year in productivity losses.[45] The *Gallup Management Journal*'s semiannual Employee Engagement Index puts the current percentage of employees who are actively disengaged at 17%. That's about 22.5 million US workers. Gallup defines *actively disengaged* as employees who are not just

unhappy in their work but who are busy acting out their unhappiness by undermining what their engaged coworkers accomplish. Each one of these angry and alienated workers is causing their employers roughly US$13,000 in yearly productivity losses on average. The study also suggests that engaged employees are not just committed or passionate or proud. They are enthusiastic and in gear, using their talents to make a difference in their employer's quest for sustainable success.

The problem of disengaged employees is not specific to the United States. For instance, a recent *Gallup* article[46] shows that in Germany, the engine of Europe's growth, one-fifth of its employees are actively disengaged, negatively affecting productivity and growth possibilities. If one also considers generational engagement, a report by Princeton-based consultants BlessingWhite[47] suggests that at least a quarter of Gen Y employees are disengaged across the globe, with the problem at its most acute in Southeast Asia, where the figure rises to around a third. These figures raise the question of whether Gen Y employees are particularly demanding, greedy and unmotivated slackers – or whether the reality is more complex. One factor that likely contributes to Millennials' more pronounced disengagement is that younger employees often do not have a clear picture of what will make them happy. That is, they often cannot find what they are looking for because they do not have sufficient experience to know what it is exactly that they want. Thus, lack of personal clarity can influence Gen Yers' lack of engagement.

The question of employee engagement is a key business issue leaders need to address, particularly in times of economic downturn and uncertainty. As a rule, the different studies and research on engagement and disengagement show that increased engagement results in increased productivity and performance. Disengaged employees, in contrast, tend to feel underutilized and disconnected from the organization's strategy and as a result may indulge in contagious negativity. Engaged employees stay for what they can give; disengaged employees stay for what they get. For the young workforce, engagement requires coherence between what is said and what is done, between what is written in the company's mission and policies and what is demonstrated by their managers. Trust in their immediate bosses and the firms' executives also appears to impact the engagement of the young workforce. Thus, consistency between a company's values, mission, strategy and daily operations is essential for companies trying to engage and commit Millennials to be a part of their workforce.

Ideas at a Glance

EVP to Support Organizational Attractiveness

- A firm's EVP comprises the firm's organizational features that allow it to promote itself outwardly and generate loyalty internally.

- Organizational features important to an EVP are the firm's organizational culture, people, work characteristics and rewards.

- Additional features that a firm has to take into account to attract and retain Millennials are

  o the social impact of the job, consistent with Gen Y's social awareness;

  o the window to the world, consistent with Millennials' ability to multitask;

  o the "me brand," consistent with the importance Millennials attach to work–life integration, multitasking and tech savvy.

NEW WAYS OF RECRUITING: THE ROLE OF SOCIAL NETWORKS

One of the main characteristics of the future organization that this book analyzes is virtuality. Being able to face and manage agile and virtual firms requires technology. However, while technology makes work more collaborative within the organization, it also poses the question of how the different generations in the workplace will adapt to a more "collaborative, connected style of work" (Salkowitz, 2008: 30). In addition, technology is presenting firms the challenge of how to use technology to attract the best talent in the market.

As Millennials are keen on the use of technology and social networks, firms are bound to use those networks as a way to reach talent by establishing a brand and building a relationship during the recruiting process. A recent survey conducted by CIPD[48] indicates that a common approach is to use Web 2.0 technologies to address the challenges of recruitment and selection (i.e., online job advertisements and application forms, online testing, digital brochures and video-based company information). P&G, for example, is an expert in the use of online applications and online testing: The first two of the five steps in its selection process – application and success drivers assessment (assesses experience and background) and reasoning screen (measures cognitive ability) – are entirely internet based.[49]

However, it should be noted that most of the technology-based techniques used today are still closer to Web 1.0 than Web 2.0, in the sense that they represent a one-way flow of information. There is an enormous and largely uncharted opportunity for organizations to apply Web 2.0 technologies to staff recruitment and selection. One only has to look at the sophisticated forums and linking mechanisms on social networking sites to realize that there is a real opportunity here. And few organizations have yet to take advantage of it.

For the future firm, it will be increasingly important to not only have an online presence but also be able to interact with prospective candidates in a way that boosts the company's brand. The reason is that when attempting to attract top talent, firms are presenting themselves and their culture to the aspirant. Attracting involves not only building adequate recruitment channels but also making sure the firm's brand is well defined and well communicated.

Ernst & Young, a pioneer in online recruiting, was among the first firms to interact with prospective candidates on Facebook. The company holds virtual roundtable discussions with members of the firm and communicates via Twitter as well. Furthermore, the company has several radio stations on Pandora. Why? "Because that's where the students are."[50]

P&G also understands the importance of communicating its brand, and in turn culture, through the use of Web 2.0 technologies. For instance, P&G allows a prospective candidate to experience the ideas behind its brand through online videos that elaborate on messages such as "we hire the person, not the position"[51] as well as through its participation in social networks such as LinkedIn and Facebook.[52]

The generational transformation plus the resulting organizational changes ahead will require that companies think about a new approach toward recruiting Millennials. This new approach should take into consideration the following dimensions: being social, being aggressively persuasive about the benefits of the firm and, finally, being a coach to prospective employees.

Being social. Being attractive in an era of agile and virtual firms requires that a firm set out a clear plan with respect to expectations and outcomes. The virtual space is so vast that companies can spend large amounts of time and money in return for little to no results if it does not carefully design its recruiting and branding strategies. But firms also need to have a social network strategy to attract and recruit young future employees.

While social networks such as Facebook and Hi5 can serve as hubs to reach the masses, a firm's social networking strategy may need to include other networks to reach its target candidates. Sites such as MySpace, YouTube and Flickr can be good places to host photos and videos aimed at niche audiences, while LinkedIn can be used to build groups, networks and discussions. Finally, a firm might use Twitter to share quick updates and links, and to promote the company through repeated interactions. Importantly, in most cases a firm's HR department will not be able to manage a firm's social networking strategy on its own. Rather, the HR department will have to collaborate with, say, the marketing department to ensure that it is successfully targeting the right people.

Another outcome of this new era of the virtual is that although many people believe this sort of exposure is neither convenient nor good, the existence of so many ways to reach people through the web can help organizations attract talent that is a good fit with the values and culture of the firm. Of course, the firm needs a clear attraction strategy; otherwise it may fail to attract the right people. Two good examples of firms that use social networks to meet the company's recruiting goals are L'Oréal and Sodexo.

L'Oréal, an international cosmetics company, is not only using social networks to identify the best young talent but is also thinking about how to update its social networking strategy to increase the firm's attractiveness to prospective employees. The company has created a Development, Trends and Intelligence department. This area explores new ways to ensure L'Oréal is attractive to the young workforce. As Gabriele Silva, recruitment project manager, observed, "L'Oréal is a very campus-, university-oriented company; this is something that is now in our DNA. We recruit much more Gen Yers than other generations."[53] Accordingly, the company is following two approaches toward being more attractive to Millennials: first, simplifying the application process for prospective candidates from this generation and, second, improving its use of social networks.

With respect to the application process, the experts at L'Oréal's Development, Trends and Intelligence department indicate that there was a need to make things easier for candidates. "Candidates now – young students – don't want to spend 20 to 25 minutes to apply [for a job at] L'Oréal . . . they are used to things that are much faster and intuitive, and our earlier application system was much more like the old school, more structured, less flexible: step 1, step 2, step 3 . . . ."[54] The changes the company has made to the application process have been significant. First, there is no longer one single portal for everybody; rather, there are now different portals for different job openings. Second, the application system is much more user-friendly, consisting of "few boxes, combined with a search button, so they can figure out how it works in two seconds: They choose, they click, that's everything they have to do."[55] As a result of these changes, the application process now takes only five to ten minutes.

Turning to the firm's use of social networks, while the company was a pioneer in participating in social networks such as Hi5 and Second Life, it knew it needed a long-term strategy where its approach toward Gen Y was concerned. Gen Y requires that it feel part of a community. With this in mind, "We are not approaching LinkedIn with just a LinkedIn approach," notes the recruitment project manager.

> We definitely know that the Facebook user of today will be a LinkedIn user in one or two years, so we always have to keep it all together. Our LinkedIn is published on our Facebook, our Facebook connects to "my personal account." When they [Gen Yers] apply, they find all the links with our social networks, so they can be part of the community just with one click.[56]

Sodexo,[57] a global leader in food service and facility management, employs a carefully designed recruitment process that incorporates the company's brand, values and culture. During this process, a candidate can find

- a traditional careers webpage;[58]

- a talent community, which is a critical resource for prospective candidates to keep abreast of the latest company news, new job openings and upcoming job fairs;[59] and

- opportunities to get involved with the company via blogs as well as Facebook, LinkedIn, Twitter and YouTube.

While in Facebook social interaction is the most important activity, Sodexo uses YouTube to introduce the firm and its activities to the community and Twitter to update the talent community about the latest company news and events. LinkedIn, however, is used by the company as a database and information channel. The company's blog is an interesting case of how to advise the younger generation about their careers while solidifying the firm's brand in the generation's mind as well. (See Figure 3.3 to understand the framework used by Sodexo in its recruitment process).

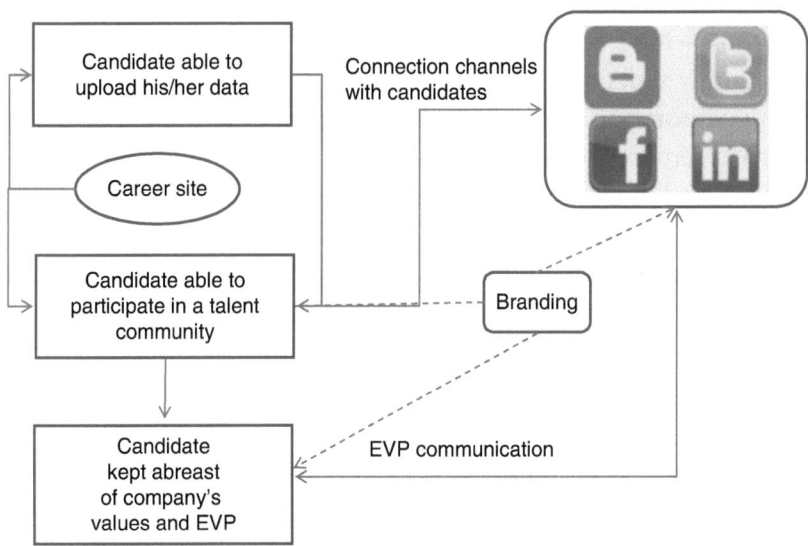

Figure 3.3 *Getting strategic about attracting Millennials: Recruiting process at Sodexo*

Being aggressively persuasive about the firm's benefits. As a prospective candidate, it is important to know the benefits that working in a particular organization can have in one's life. We have already discussed Gen Yers' main characteristics and interests. When communicating about an opportunity, a company should speak to these generational characteristics and interests to make the company more attractive and entice the younger generation to apply for the opportunity. But communicating about how a company appeals to these features will be effective only when this message reflects the reality at the firm. For example, firms that limit the possibility of flextime or flexible schedules should not speak to such benefits if they do not really and truly offer them. Being attractive may therefore require a change in paradigm and culture to adapt the firm to meet the expectations of the future generations.

In some markets, particularly in Asia, global firms are extending awareness of their brands as employers in an aggressive way by building a relationship between themselves and their employees' families. For example, Motorola – the telecommunication company – and Nestlé – a leading nutrition, health and wellness company – have tried to strengthen these links in China through their family visits and family day initiatives. Aditya Birla, a US$40 billion corporation in Mumbai, India, webcasts its annual employee award ceremony to all employees and their families around the world. "And in all markets, companies are likely to find that many young, aspiring managers view being part of a broader cause and contributing to their countries' overall economic development as increasingly important" (Dewhurst et al., 2012: 2).[60]

AMC Theatres,[61] a company with 361 theaters and more than 5,000 screens across the United States and Canada, knows how to attract young candidates to work with them. Employee benefits include free movies, flexible schedules and fun.[62] Another company that aggressively works to attract new young employees is Zappos,[63] an American online shoe retailer. The company makes its offices open to the world by virtue of an "Inside Zappos"[64] Twitter account. Through this communication channel as well as its videos and blogs, the company offers not only fun but also insight into what it is like working with the firm and the firm's social and community activities. Zappos's founder, Tony Hsieh, emphasizes that one of his goals is to "increase the number of serendipitous interactions of our staff, inside and outside the firm."[65] At Zappos, dating among employees is even encouraged as such a policy is consistent with valuing this generation's interest in work–life integration.

Clif Bar & Co is a leading producer of organic bars. The company seeks to serve five groups: the planet, the community, the firm's people, the business and the firm's brands.[66] Consistent with these aims, the firm implemented an Employee Stock Ownership Plan (ESOP) and offers financial incentives for energy-efficient home improvements (the company itself installed the largest smart solar array in the country) and for purchasing hybrid or biodiesel vehicles. The result, as Gergen and Vanourek (2009) observe, is that the company is regarded a hot place to work in the San Francisco area.

While it might be easier for some companies to tailor a set of benefits specific to the younger generation of employees, the challenge for such firms is to make sure they are providing an appropriate set of benefits for each of the different generations in the organization (see Figure 3.4). Furthermore, the firm should make clear why it offers different benefits packages to different generations at the firm, so that employees recognize the attractiveness of the benefits they are offered.

Consistent with the above arguments, a recent report by Hyphen[67] shows that firms need to adopt a flexible approach to compensation and benefits so that they will be able to satisfy the different priorities of the different generations. While previous generations might have been delighted with a pension plan, making a company offering pensions attractive, Hyphen shows that only 4% of the younger workforce is attracted to a firm for this reason. Given the recent turmoil in financial markets worldwide, it may be the case that while pension plans were previously synonymous with stability, a quality that was desirable by job seekers, today's younger employees consider them unstable and hence not particularly valuable.

According to the study by Hyphen, the younger workforce seek flexible benefits that can be tailored to their individual needs. Flexible holidays, time off on top of annual leave and additional time off between Christmas and New Years are considered critical to Millennials. Hyphen's survey found that 25% of 16- to 24-year-olds chose their employer based on the number of paid holidays. In addition, 11% of this group indicated that it was attracted to employers that hold social events.

Figure 3.4 *Finding the right set of benefits for each generation*

Dow is an American firm with an industry-leading portfolio of specialty chemicals, advanced materials, agrosciences and plastics businesses. It provides a broad range of technology-based products and solutions to customers in approximately 160 countries. In 2011, Dow had annual sales of US$53.7 billion and employed approximately 52,000 people worldwide.[68] At Dow, the notion of total rewards or EVP has been present for quite some time, which suggests that employee benefits include much more than just a salary. "In today's labor market, where the presence of Generation Y employees is growing significantly," comments Sebastián Soria, global compensation director at Dow, looking at the broader picture of rewards has become even more critical. Let's be clear: competitive compensation and benefits has and will continue to be critical in attracting and retaining top talent. However, for Gen Y financial gains are not the primary reason to join or stay with an employer. This generation needs to feel a connection with a larger purpose, represented by the company's mission, vision and values. Their demand for flexibility, sustainability and feeling like part of a great team are some of their defining features.[69]

Currently, Dow is in the process of revamping its EVP and communication strategy to make sure both current and prospective employees fully understand the broad spectrum of benefits the company offers. The new theme will be "solutionism," which refers to Dow being a solution provider for some of the planet's main challenges. Among other target outcomes of this re-branding is to maximize the impact of the company's benefits and EVP to Millennials.

A more compelling study by Cisco[70] shows that firms need to have a well-thought strategy for attracting the young workforce that is both persuasive and aggressive in how it communicates the benefits the firm offers. The study, conducted in 14 countries and based on the responses of more than 3,000 college students (18- to 24-year-olds) and "end users" (21- to 29-year-olds), shows that when presented a job offer at a company that is inflexible with respect to accessing social media, 56% of job candidates would decline the offer. Furthermore, for at least 33% of respondents, the benefits most likely to lead them to accept a job offer are flexibility in technology choice, access to social media and the option to work remotely. In particular, 33% of respondents indicate they consider a company's policy with respect to the use of mobile phone devices and social media at work when deciding whether to accept or reject a job offer, and almost half of the respondents indicate that they would consider accepting a lower paid job offer if working remotely and having freedom to use mobile phone devices were part of the package.

Based on the above discussion, it will be increasingly important for a firm to create an aggressively persuasive benefits strategy that considers the best mix of benefits for the different generations in its workforce, and the firm's ability to provide such benefits, to make sure that the different generations in its organization get similarly attractive benefits that are tailored to their specific needs.

Being a coach to prospective employees. The recruiting process needs to not only attract the attention of the new generation of workers but also help them understand the nature of the job opportunities available. It is increasingly the case that the younger workforce reaches the stage of going out to get a job without a clear idea of what they want to do or how organizations work. Millennials have an idealistic vision of the kind of places they want to work in and the kind of work they want to do. However, they are lagging behind in terms of understanding how that vision translates into day-to-day operations. Therefore, more and more firms are focusing not only on attracting Millennials but also on helping them learn about the company and showing them the different possibilities for development and growth in different areas of the organization. How do firms do this? Again, we find examples in the marketplace.

McDonald's, for instance, offers interview tips on their career website. The idea behind such tips is that they can help increase the likelihood that applicants will arrive prepared for interviews. Some of the tips on the company's website include plan ahead, be on time, watch what you wear, sell yourself with facts, be positive and so on.[71]

L'Oréal has created a platform called "L'Oréal & Me." This platform elaborates on the job offer, the value proposition, the recruitment process, the way the firm integrates people into the company and the way the firm manages employees' careers, and thus makes the entire application and selection process much more transparent than in the past.[72] This platform also has longer term benefits in that, once the young employees are working in the company, they are prepared for transparency in decision-making, which strengthens the dialog between managers and their teams and boosts employees' involvement in their career development. Once on board, coaching is key to facilitate the successful integration of the new employee. The FIT program (Follow-Up and Integration Track) is a two-year personalized guidance and training program. FIT provides six learning opportunities for the young employee[73]:

1. A personalized welcome, during which special attention is given to developing a positive, committed relationship with each new employee.

2. Introduction to the field and the company's products, two fundamental sources of inspiration and ideas.

3. Training and roundtable discussions, which are critical for passing on knowledge and expertize, fostering the exchange of ideas and networking.

4. A personalized meeting program, which allows the young employee to quickly learn about the working environment and the challenges involved.

5. On-the-job learning supported by line management, which gives the new employee opportunities to learn from multiple professional situations.

6. Individual guidance from mentors and HR, which helps the new employees focus on where they are in the organization and how to develop their careers within the group.

In addition to FIT, online job boards highlighting updated career opportunities and the HR intranet portal are now available in all countries in which the company operates. These continually updated resources help ensure that all employees can access the full range of career development possibilities and services the company offers, including the online employee appraisal system and the new digital learning platform, My Learning.

At L'Oréal, job coaching does not come down to a one-shot event in which a prospective candidate is introduced to available job opportunities, and then, when hired, the process ends. On the contrary, coaching is a continuous process that begins with the candidate being oriented to possible experiences within the firm and continues after the candidate is hired, so that the new employee has a soft landing upon entering a corporate life and feels committed to the process. L'Oréal therefore coaches both candidates and employees, accompanying them throughout their professional development.[74]

Future Trends: The Helicopter Parents[75]

> Employer alert: Helicopter parents are whirring into the workplace. Helicopter parents feel that their kids are living in a very competitive world right now, starting in college in which competition is intense for getting the best chances. These parents feel that they have to do everything they can to give their kids a leg up against their competitors, whether that means helping them prepare for college term exams, complaining about a teacher who doesn't give them a fair grade or getting involved in the workplace, not only helping their kids get ready for the job but also actually being part of the job interview and salary negotiations. So they really have gone over the edge!
>
> After a lot of interviews with the parents of this generation, it is clear that they see their children as a reflection of themselves; in other words, their children's success makes them look like great parents, which motivates them to be more involved in their kids' lives. Parents view their children as trophies: Their kids' success is their success. Thus, parents are, to some degree, taking responsibility for their kids' success.

It is not surprising, then, to see that parents are getting involved in the workplace. They are trying to get information on companies for their kids. They are trying to sit in on job interviews with their kids. I have even heard of a case when, after a young person was hired and received a bad performance review, the parents called the manager and complained! It's a very bizarre situation to see parents involved so late in their children's life.

These situations are happening more and more and managers in large companies who have never seen parents trying some of these things are starting to see them now. The most bizarre case I have heard involved Fedex, the package delivery company: A candidate's parents wanted to sit in on their child's interview and also wanted Fedex to pay their travel expenses to the company's offices. Their demands as helicopter parents can be quite amazing and help explain why Millennials have such high expectations and unrealistic demands.

Ideas at a Glance

Attracting Millennials into the Workplace

- In agile and virtual firms, social networks and technology will shape how firms organize and compete in the future.

- Social networks and technology are also critical for reaching and attracting talent.

- Recruiting Millennials will require that firms consider the following dimensions:

    o being social, to attract the right young talent;

- being aggressively persuasive regarding the benefits of the firm and, in particular, about how the benefits are in line with Millennials' interests;
- being a coach to prospective employees, helping them understand the nature of the job and guiding them through the recruitment process.

Questions for Managers

- Does your company have the right EVP for today's market?
  - Does your EVP enhance the firm's ability to communicate with, attract and retain young talent?
  - What are the main organizational dimensions your firm should be working on to enhance the effectiveness of its EVP?
- Is your company offering a valuable brand, jobs with social impact or the possibility to enhance the employability of young employees?
- Is your firm using social networks and technology in the recruitment process?
  - Are these tools being used effectively?
- Does your organization offer a set of benefits that is tailored to the needs and interests of the new generation?
- Is your firm guiding prospective employees through the recruitment process, helping candidates get to know the nature of the job and company's aims?

CASE IN POINT: "REVEAL" BY L'ORÉAL, ATTRACTING MILLENNIALS AND GUIDING THEM INTO THE WORKPLACE

L'Oréal is a cosmetics company headquartered in France with over a century of expertize. The company had approximately €20.3 billion consolidated sales in 2011 based on 27 global brands with a presence in 130 countries, and accounts for 68,900 employees.[76]

L'Oréal is not a newcomer in terms of creating tools to attract Millennials. Rather, the company has been a first mover by employing online simulations and games such as e-Strat, Brandstorm, Innovation Lab, Ingenius and Sales (Hatum, 2010). Each of these games was designed to a specific audience that the firm wanted to attract. "Reveal," however, is a different concept. This is more than a business game. It is a unique simulation experience that any student preparing to embark on a professional life is invited to participate in, regardless of his or her academic background.

In a Web 2.0 world[77] where virtual and real lives are mixed, each participant assumes the role of a management trainee who has just arrived at L'Oréal and is pulled into an incredible cosmetics innovation adventure. This leads the individual to meet many key players from business fields such as R&D, finance, operations, marketing and business development. Over the course of the game's situational exercises, participants *reveal* their talents while learning about the company's culture.

Image showing some of the virtual characters of Reveal, L'Oréal's online product innovation simulation.
Image courtesy of the company. Used with permission.

Why would L'Oréal invest in the development of Reveal if the company had already created a series of business games to attract Millennials? "This is because Gen Y needs to be oriented," explains Aude Desanges, Talent Recruitment International.

> This generation needs to be oriented by professors, but also by the companies, meaning that we think we have a mission to help them see exactly what they can do in a

company regardless of their academic background. Gen Y is our inspiration; they think "I want to do everything," that is the student speech, but "I don't know what to do and I don't know where to start in my career, and I want to do so many things because I am so curious, because I am a Gen Y, and I am full of ambition, but I don't know what a global company is exactly, what kind of activities exist."[78]

So the company wanted to help Millennials discover what kind of careers they can have in a global company such as L'Oréal. "We wanted to answer the questions, 'what are you up for, what you are good at, what is it exactly that you want to do.' Normally, they don't know what to do."[79]

"Reveal is the best understanding we could get of this new generation," continues Francois de Wazières, director of International Recruitment,

> to get a tool that matches what they desire in life, to get a tool that plays on their ambitions, on their flexibility, on the way they see their professional life as something very open, where we don't want to see any clusters, like "I studied engineering, I must be an engineer." With Reveal, we played on their willingness to escape from boundaries and be more on a quest of ambition for themselves.[80]

Once the game has been completed, participants receive a personalized evaluation. The best participants may be invited by HR teams in their country to a "B-Revealed" event, where they spend two days at a local L'Oréal office to get hands-on experience working with L'Oréal, network with business professionals from different business areas and meet with recruiters. "For us Reveal is a sourcing tool, a complementary sourcing tool. The recruiters can identify the best participants, check their CVs, select the best candidates and organize B-Revealed events."[81] From the recruiter's point of view, this tool also improves the interview with the job candidate. After participating in the

Reveal simulation, candidates are able to ask the right questions and apply for the right position.

> [While before] it was really frustrating from the recruiter's point of view as well as from the candidate's because candidates were asking basic questions, and the recruiter and the candidate were both wasting their time. But the candidate did not know much about the company or what the company wanted. With Reveal, we are providing the candidate with a particular experience, after which they know what they want to ask – a win-win situation.[82]

The simulation game also allows HR to evaluate something else that is important to the company: the extent to which the job candidate is likely to be a good fit for the company. The idea is that at the end of the simulation, the best scores represent the best profiles for L'Oréal, meaning not only the best in a given field but also the best in terms of the company's culture and values. Reveal therefore helps recruiters answer the questions: "Do they fit with L'Oréal? Would they be happy in our culture?"[83] According to the interviewees, the right people for L'Oréal are very curious, have an international outlook, love to work in a team, enjoy being challenged and challenging others, are innovative and are able to defend their opinions.

The ultimate goal for candidates who participate in a Reveal simulation is to have better knowledge of themselves and their talents, to have a good idea of the career opportunities offered by L'Oréal and to have a chance to join the group. For L'Oréal, this experience is key to attracting the right talent for its businesses, particularly with respect to the Millennial generation.

4
New Learning Paradigms and the Challenge of Developing the Future Leaders

THE NEW PARADIGMS OF LEARNING

One of the most significant changes Millennials are bringing to organizations is the fact that they learn in a different way. This poses a real challenge to any organization in terms of how to teach and develop this generation to release the potential of the young workforce.

When describing the way this generation learns, Elmore (2010) uses the term EPIC: experiential, participatory, image-rich and connected. According to Elmore, experience is all-important to these youngsters and hence teaching and communication should avoid relying only on lectures; that is, it should be more interactive. Participation is also important to this generation, as the young Millennials commonly express themselves by uploading what they feel and think on the internet. In addition, Gen Yers are image-rich; that is, this generation is accustomed to using verbal as well as visual symbols to express themselves, and it finds stimulation from images. Last, but not least, this generation is connected both socially and technologically.

The EPIC young workforce has entered the classroom. They arrived on campus with their iPod plugged into one ear and Bluetooth in the other, sending instant messages to some friends while updating their status on Facebook and uploading pictures.

And ah! when they have spare time, they may be found studying or working on assignments for their courses. But what sort of context have they found upon arriving in the classroom? – an old-fashioned classroom full of chairs directed toward a blackboard or whiteboard on which a teacher (hopefully he or she is not too bored) is writing without stopping for a breath. In the meantime the Millennial students are bored to death, texting each other and using computers for purposes unrelated to what is going on in the classroom. Left-brain schools in a right brain world is the sentence used by Elmore (2010:176) to summarize this situation. Workplace learning, then, should be considered a competitive advantage for every company. People need to learn quickly and not just on the rare occasion when they are in a classroom.

According to Tapscott (2009), the Net Geners, as he calls Millennials, have grown up in a digital world and yet, while they are living in the twenty-first century, their education system in many instances is lagging behind at least 100 years. Why is Tapscott so negative about the education system? He argues that "[t]he model of education that still prevails today was designed for the Industrial Age. It revolves around the teacher who delivers a one-size-fits-all, one-way lecture. The student, working alone, is expected to absorb the content delivered by the teacher" (2009: 122). If we analyze students' schedules in many schools worldwide, we can see that Tapscott's observations are correct. Students are running from one class to the next every 45 minutes. During a single morning, they can be subjected to lectures on as many as three or four subjects, from math to biology, memorizing formulas, thinking about how the cellular system works and perhaps also trying to understand a Shakespearean or other classic text. Moreover, as Tapscott observes, "Each time, the learning is interrupted by that bell" (2009: 122).

D'Angelo (2009) asks a critical question of today's educators: How can teachers better teach Gen Yers? She acknowledges the importance of including peer teaching and tutoring into the mix to be successful not only in terms of understanding the material at hand but also in terms of retaining information. This is important for a generation that is good at teamwork and experiential activities, and that is accustomed to technology being incorporated into their learning. In D'Angelo's view, Millennials are less interested in accumulating knowledge and facts and are instead more results oriented. She points out that if Gen Yers can put together a report using online resources that allows them to collaborate with others they might be happier and more efficient.

Knapp (2009) supports D'Angelo's ideas, stating that Millennials are used to group projects and assignments and enjoy a stronger peer-group dynamic than prior generations. This means that Gen Yers care a lot about what their friends think, and they look for recommendations from them. Under this peer-group dynamic, constant feedback from friends reinforces the logic of socially networked resources such as Google, Wikipedia, YouTube and so on. The problem today, then, is that educators traditionally sell the idea that the best information comes from experts, while Millennials rely on social networking sites to obtain input, share concerns and be convinced by peers.

The fact that the way people learn has evolved from a teacher-centered, one-size-fits-all methodology toward a learner-centered, one-size-fits-one (Tapscott, 2009) methodology is relevant for organizations that would like to create effective learning and development programs. Out is instruction, and in is mentoring and discovering. Learning should no longer be individualistic but rather collaborative.

Millennials are also strong believers in lifelong learning. The workplace will thus be increasingly expected to provide learning opportunities, which means organizations will have to adjust to try to meet Millennials' demands and questions regarding the learning possibilities offered by the organization.

So, what is happening at the organizational level? How can the changes in the way people learn affect organizations? The impact of individual learning is critical for organizational learning and the knowledge produced at the organizational level. Illeris (2011) suggests that the dominant approach toward learning at the workplace today is the human resource management approach or human resource management development. While this point of view stresses the importance of human conditions, it is a management approach rather than a learning approach in Illeris's opinion. This means that learning is viewed from management, organizational and financial perspectives. Argyris and Schön (1999) introduce the idea of organizational learning. According to these authors, learning has a central position in organizations that recognize that people and not the organization itself learn. However, they offer a workplace-related contribution to the theory on learning as people can learn within organizations (single-loop and double-loop learning).

Highlighting the extensive learning that takes place incidentally through work, Illeris (2011) proposes the concept of work-based learning or workplace learning. Under this view, learning is a social process that takes place between people, not only in people. This view further stresses that the learning culture or environment is critical for the learning process.

Bingham and Conner (2010) also emphasize the importance of social learning. Social media are technologies used to engage three or more people, and social learning involves participating with others to make sense of information and generate new ideas. What is new according to the authors is the powerful effect social media have on social learning. It thus appears that the benefits of social learning are augmented by different social media tools such as Facebook, Twitter, YouTube, blogs and wikis.

Based on the above discussion, it is clear that firms have to be aware of the impact people, and in particular Millennials, are going to have on their organizations in terms of their need to learn in a dynamic, experiential and collaborative fashion, and people are going to need to acknowledge the value of a corporate and organizational culture that allows them to learn, collaborate and interact. The learning process, then, will require the interaction between organizations and their employees. Table 4.1 shows the implications for organizations of Millennial's learning process.

At the organizational level, learning can be differentiated between formal and informal. Van Dam (2011) describes formal learning as structured, curriculum-driven and role- or level-based learning that is formulated by an organization. In other words, the organization determines what kind of learning needs to happen over a specific

Table 4.1 *Millennials' characteristics and the learning process*

Millennials' characteristics	How Millennials learn	Implications for organizations
Work-life integration	• Millennials integrate technology and social networks into their daily routine. They do not differentiate spaces for learning. They are learning and interacting all the time	• Learning should be integrated into their activities and be based on technology and social networks. Collaborative learning is critical for success
Multitasking	• They avoid a single focus and prefer a multi-focus way of learning	• Different technologies and learning methods are necessary to ensure good results. It is important to provide customized learning rather than one-size-fits-all learning. Interactive learning opportunities are required
Tech savvy	• Technology is all-important to their learning success. They need access to technology and social networks to learn. They do not like instructions, prefer trial and error	• Access to social networks is necessary in the workplace. Implement state-of-the-art technology to make learning interesting. Allow them to follow a discovery journey
Social awareness	• Does not apply	• Does not apply

time frame for employees to develop pre-identified competences. Formal learning can be delivered in a classroom context (physical or virtual), through self-paced e-learning programs or through online diagnostic and assessment tools.

Informal learning, however, can be defined as semistructured or unstructured learning that is driven by the daily learning and development needs of employees and occurs on the job through problem-solving, interaction with colleagues and the use of the internet.

Van Dam (2011) further distinguishes three types of informal learning: career-driven learning, on-demand learning and social learning.

Career-driven learning. Most learning takes place when people move into different roles and/or work on new projects where they are moving outside their "comfort zone" into a new area – "the learning zone." These experiences are most effective if they are supported by on-the-job coaching and mentoring, and supplemented with formal learning programs (e.g., an executive MBA).

On-demand learning. People are constantly looking for knowledge and information that helps them perform their jobs. The internet, search engines, electronic performance support systems and mobile computing all provide people access to content on a 24/7 basis, which help them fill knowledge gaps.

Social learning. Social learning refers to people effectively interacting with others about a given topic. This form of group interaction seems to engage people around a collaborative, alternative style of learning. Content is no longer developed by just the corporate learning and development departments. Instead, the end user (employee) helps develop content and share this information within his or her network.

The learning experience allows people and organizations to try approaches ranging from the more traditional classroom experience (i.e., formal learning) to more complex, collaborative and social types of learning (i.e., informal learning), which include tools such as wikis, blogs, micro-blogging, social networks, game-based learning, virtual coaching and mentoring.

Companies need to make sure that the learning process they implement is the right one for them. Today companies have to attract Millennials and make sure they are integrated into the organization. Moreover, these Millennials want to work in a collaborative environment, move fast the ladder quickly and restructure the way organizations work. Everything is fast for this generation but firms need to make sure they can provide the right learning and development that a professional needs to build a growing and sustainable career.

In his book *Outliers, the Story of Success*, Malcom Gladwell (2008) repeatedly refers to the "10,000-hour rule," according to which the key to success in any field is, to a large extent, a matter of practicing a specific task for a total of approximately 10,000 hours. This means ten years working 20 hours a week on a specific task. This may be too much for the fast-paced Gen Y. However, if the 10,000-hour rule well captures the only way a person can really achieve expertize in a specific discipline, this raises the question of how organizations can balance the haste required by Millennials against the gradualness needed to acquire expertize. A firm's ultimate learning strategy should likely allow for different paces, incorporate the use of different technologies and aim to develop different types of competencies.

In an attempt to help organizations create a learning strategy for the new generation of workers, Figure 4.1 summarizes the different approaches toward learning today.

Based on the matrix introduce in Figure 4.1, companies need to bear in mind that the workplace and everything surrounding the workplace (i.e., courses, networks, contact with customers and suppliers etc.) is where the learning process can take place. The learning context provided by the organization will determine the learning opportunities available to employees. Aspects of the learning context include the technology used and the degree of access provided to different sources of knowledge. Of course, as Illeris (2011) points out, there is also potential learning, or what is called individual potential learning, because it is the person who has the potential to learn and take advantage of the opportunities to learn.

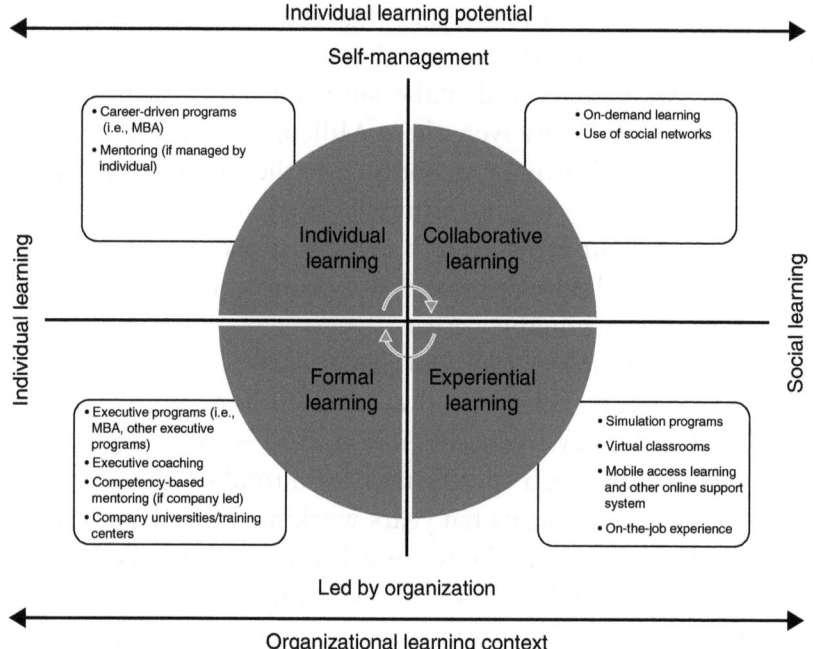

Figure 4.1 *Learning strategy matrix*

The above matrix comprises four dimensions that, when combined, represent the different ways that organizations and people can learn: self-managed learning, organization-led learning, individual learning and social learning. The combination of these dimensions, as discussed previously, leads to four learning strategies: individual learning, formal learning, experiential learning and collaborative learning.

Individual learning includes, among other things, those activities that are important for one's own career, such as pursuing an MBA to acquire the knowledge and flavor of corporate management practices. *Formal learning*, which is organized by firms and oriented toward the acquisition of specific managerial or technical competencies, includes traditional training courses, courses taught under the umbrella of companies' universities, campuses or trainee centers (e.g., the Accenture Leadership Center[1] or Deloitte University[2]), executive programs as well as executive coaching.

Experiential learning comprises learning opportunities organized by firms that involve the use of more sophisticated technological tools to enhance the learning process. Virtual classrooms, simulations and technological devices that reach different people at different locations are included in this category. Experiential learning also includes the more traditional approach known as on-the-job training.

Finally, *collaborative learning* is an individually led approach toward skills development that is on demand, where people can access instructional materials whenever they choose, and in a participatory and community-driven way, which means that individuals exchange knowledge and ideas with other people inside or outside the organization. This boundaryless approach includes people gaining knowledge or information through, for example, social networks.

The foregoing matrix sheds some light on what has historically been the best learning strategy for different generations and what may be the best learning strategy for Millennials. During the time when baby boomers were the most relevant generation in organizations, learning processes focused on individual, formal and experiential learning, where the latter included on-the-job training as a way to increase job expertize. This appears to have been enough for both people and firms for a number of years. As Gen Xers entered the fold, technological advancements led companies to incorporate more sophisticated tools in their experiential learning program, tools that became critical for the learning and development process. Simulations and virtual classrooms emerged as interesting approaches toward learning.

An example of a firm combining collaborative and experiential learning is BP. BP is one of the world's largest energy companies, employing more than 80,000 people worldwide and offering products and services in more than 100 countries.[3]

In 2009, BP explored new territory in virtual learning by using 3-D virtual worlds, social networking tools and collaboration-based approaches to meet the development needs of their 400+ new graduate hires during their second year with BP. Van Dam (2011) describes the methods applied by BP. One of these methods is

Global Graduate Village, a 3-D virtual campus where new hires work in teams across geographies and segments to complete learning assignments. In the Global Graduate Village challenge, teams comprising ten new graduate hires imagine that they are BP's executive team in the year 2025. They are tasked with evaluating the current business environment, considering a variety of business strategies and making recommendations with respect to the path forward. Participants create virtual representations of themselves by creating an individual profile and designing a personal avatar. The avatar represents the participant virtually in the 3-D world. A 2-D profile with photographs, key information, experience and interests helps support the identity of the participant in the virtual world. Over a four-week period, the teams attend live learning sessions with subject matter experts, including some of the firm's most senior leaders, and have access to supporting self-study learning materials. The teams can also use the social networking tools available in the platform, such as application sharing, online messaging and voice over internet protocol (VoIP), to meet online and collaborate on their assignments.

Another company focusing on collaborative and experiential learning is Lastminute.com (http://www.lastminute.com). Lastminute.com is the United Kingdom's leading online travel and leisure retailer, with over 1.65 million visitors per week. The company sold 750,000 airline tickets to 1,300 destinations worldwide in 2010 and has received many awards in the travel, tourism and leisure industry.[4]

Marko Balabanovic, head of innovation at Lastminute.com, leads teams tasked with developing projects that are more experimental. In his view, the importance that the company places on learning helps make Lastminute.com successful not only in terms of running the business and anticipating competitors but also in terms of incorporating the new young workforce into the firm:

> First of all, we allow people to spend time learning new things. This is critical for us, learning. . . . If we need to learn about a certain new technology we allocate time to it, and we'll make sure we have books and whatever

other support is needed. We will set up sessions so that people can present to the rest of the team all about this new thing.[5]

Alex Duncan, the head of online development, continues, "This is a very good place to learn because it's a very complicated technical environment to work in, it's difficult. So, anyone who comes in here will learn a lot."[6]

During my visit at Lastminute.com, Balabanovic's team was working on a new system to book on a very last minute basis, in particular theater tickets on the same day of the show. Balabanovic explains that this project highlights the importance of collaboration and experiential learning for success with the young workforce:

> For us this project is a reasonably big one because we have to create a new relationship with the theaters and box offices. But at the same time, we have to think about the system from the customers' point of view, when will they use such a system, how will they find it, how does it work etc. So with the team in charge of the project we rented a room right by Leicester Square, which is where the theater district is. We spent a few hours there brainstorming and then split up into teams, and we went out and everybody had to try and buy a theater ticket using a different mechanism. Some people had to do it on the web, some people had to use mobile phones and some people had to go to half-price booths or to the box office at the theater. So we did it in many different ways, all the time taking photos and videos, trying to observe what was good, what was bad. When we came back, we discussed our observations and started to create. That kind of day would be very hard to justify in a strict kind of way, but without that kind of time you'd never really understand the problem you're trying to solve, and you could end up building something that doesn't work very well for the customer.[7]

For young Millennials, this hands-on approach to learning that also involves teaming up with their colleagues seems to be critical for being effective, on the one hand, and for motivating them, on the other.

> What we are doing is making sure that everybody on the team is brought into the design process. This motivates the young generation a lot. In the end, we want people to be motivated so that when we launch the product, they can say, "I did that, and I'm proud of that. That's my team, we built that thing." That's what I want to create, an environment where people can take a personal kind of pride in the thing they've done.[8]

Experience and collaboration allows the young workforce to get involved and to sort out technical or work-related problems in an efficient way.

Lastminute.com is also exploring the use of what it refers to as "hack days." A hack day is an event where developers, designers and people with ideas gather to create "cool stuff." Yahoo! Developer Network hosts one of the most prominent and well-known hack days.[9] At Lastminute.com, employees are given 24 hours to create new tools or products and then show them off. "Some people stay overnight; it is kind of a frenzy atmosphere that day. We get some food, people start working intensively on some idea; whatever it is, it doesn't have to be related to their jobs. And then they get 90 seconds to show us all what they have created."[10]

> Motivation; experience doing what you want; trying new things, technology or tools that you didn't have a chance to do in your normal work; and the opportunity for someone who might be very junior in the company to show off how good they are to someone like the CEO who might be watching are the drivers of this activity.[11]

Figure 4.2 summarizes the different approaches toward learning and Millennials' preference.

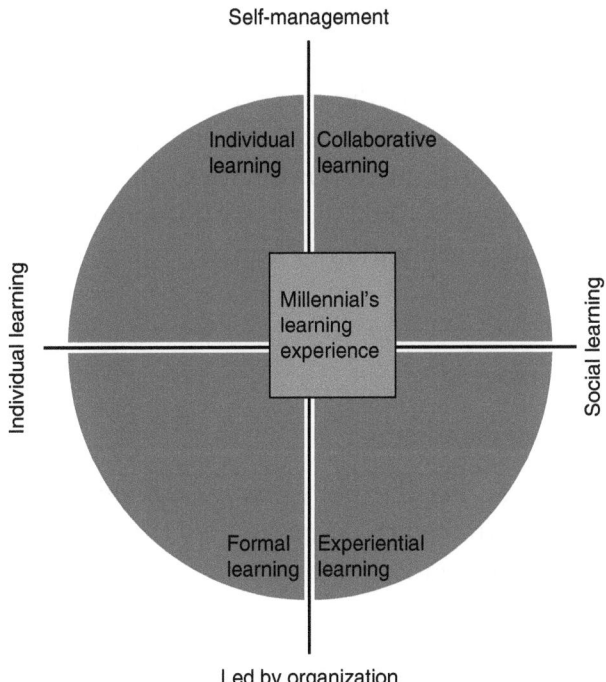

Figure 4.2 *Learning experience for Millennials*

Millennials are definitively different. Not only does this generation have an approach toward life and work that is dissimilar to that of other generations, but Gen Yers also have been heavily influenced by technologies that have changed the way we work and relate to each other. Individuals and hence organizations are no longer sufficiently served only by formal training. Different backgrounds and learning styles, as well as the complexity of people's jobs, should now determine how people learn. In the hyper-social organization, as Gossieaux and Moran (2010) call today's organizations, the role of social networks is significant for Millennials. It is not difficult to see, therefore, that the collaboration dimension in the matrix of Figure 4.2 is not only relevant but also critical for any organization wanting to build capabilities through Gen Yers. Thus, firms have to encourage incidental learning, learning from interacting with others, and learning as an outcome of doing one's work. The collaborative dimension allows people to become developers of content, sharing this new content with their network. At the same time, however, organizations need to overcome the inexperience of a generation that wants to grow fast but does not have sufficient experience to take over more important responsibilities. This issue leads us to the following section, a topic that is critical for all organizations, developing the next generation of leaders.

Ideas at a Glance

New Learning Paradigms

- *Experiential, participatory, image-rich* and *connected* are words frequently used to describe the approach Millennials have toward learning.

- The learning experience can be individual, formal, experiential and/or collaborative according to whether the learning process is led by the organization or the individual (self-managed) and whether it is shaped by individual or social learning.

- The impact of the changes in the way people learn has important implications for organizations that need to adapt their learning activities to make sure they can build the capabilities required to be competitive and successful in the future. Collaborative learning is highly relevant for Gen Yers and thus needs to be incorporated into firms' portfolio of learning activities.

DEVELOPING THE NEXT GENERATION OF LEADERS

What will be the leader of the future be like? Answering this question is critical to understand how organizations need to prepare and develop the young generation for future leadership positions. There is no certain answer to this question, however, just an educated guess. Why is this issue relevant? Because Millennials maybe thrust into leadership positions at a younger age than previous generations were, as there are not enough Gen Xers to fill all leadership and critical roles left by retiring baby boomers. Sujansky and Ferri-Reed state that the future success of the Millennials will be dependent upon how they are groomed for future leaders (2009: 141).

Many authors have referred to what is today an open question regarding what future leaders will be like; that is, of what will be the main competencies and characteristics of those with the responsibility to organize and strategize in the years to come. Is the future leader completely different from today's leaders?

In their book *The Leadership Machine*, Lombardo and Eichinger (2001) argue that four fundamentals are not likely to change much. These are the competencies and skills that matter for leading in new and different situations, how those skills are acquired and developed, who is equipped to learn these skills and what it takes to make skills development work. The question, then, is how the new generation of future leaders will fit in terms of the four fundamentals described by the authors above. We have discussed throughout the book how organizations are becoming more agile and virtual and how the new young workforce is bringing a new set of strengths and interests into organizations. In addition, we have discussed how Gen Yers clearly have different needs in terms of the learning process. The four fundamentals described by Lombardo and Eichner are thus likely to be different for Millennials.

The million-dollar question is: *how* will the next generation of leaders be different. While we cannot predict exactly how the future will be, we can make an educated guess based on what we have learned so far about Gen Y's learning capabilities, attitudes and skills. Figure 4.3 summarizes this information into a simple diagram.

The agile and virtual firms that are described throughout this book have transformed themselves through a process of organizational

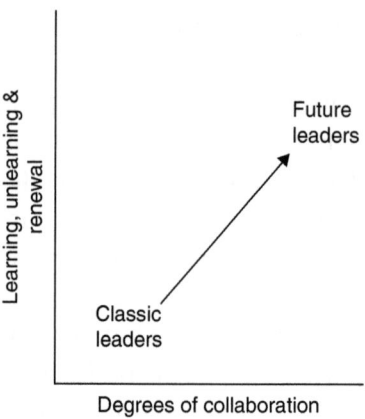

Figure 4.3 *Leaders of the future*

and strategic renewal. Floyd and Lane (2000) describe renewal as an iterative process of beliefs, action and learning with the purpose of aligning the organization and its strategy with changing environmental circumstances.

Volberda et al. (2001) introduce the concept of transformational renewal to refer to those transformations at the organizational and individual levels that are associated with significant unlearning, new ways of thinking and different technological paths. According to Volberda and his colleagues, a transformational renewal journey is characterized by periods of systemic exploration as the organization and its people renew and update their skills and competencies. Similarly, Rindova and Kotha's (2001) analysis of what they call "continuous morphing" in two internet firms reveals that firms in a continuous state of transformation ("morphing") are able to regenerate competitive advantages when competitive conditions changed. Being agile and flexible, and having the right people, facilitates such transformations.

Therefore, based on today's organizational transformation, it seems that learning, unlearning and renewal will be three dimensions of future leaders' lives. The young generation entering the workplace is very keen on continued learning and does not mind unlearning and renewing themselves to adapt to the context in which they are embedded.

The dimension of collaboration in Figure 4.3 has been already discussed above. The new generation is looking forward to collaborating in the different dimensions of their work life. Millennials prefer collaborative ways of learning, shared office spaces and letting people participate in decision-making.

The combination of the capacities to learn, unlearn and renew, on the one hand, and to collaborate, on the other, will form the basis of the future leader. This future leader will have new competencies relative to today's corporate leaders. McCarthy (2009) lists some of the skills that this generation is bringing to work and that will deepen over time: shared leadership, with the future leader developing strong teams and giving power away; technological mastery, with new technologies bringing new business opportunities and new ways to solve organizational problems; partnering, with future leaders collaborating, building coalitions and mastering empathy to be able to come up with creative solutions.

Goldsmith (2008) posits that those qualities of future leaders that will be distinct from those of current leaders are as follows: global leadership, cross-cultural appreciation, technological savvy, tendency to build alliances and partnerships and shared leadership. Hamel and Breen (2007) also suggest that leadership will become increasingly distributed.

One of the most detailed analyzes on future leadership capabilities and competencies is that by Meister and Willyerd (2010), who conclude their research with a five-dimensional framework of the 2020 leader. According to Meister and Willyerd, future leaders will first demonstrate a collaborative mind-set, working comfortably with others and being inclusive and participative in the decision-making process. Second, they will be masters of developing people and will be able to mentor, give feedback and provide career guidance effectively. Third, they will be digitally confident, using technology to connect both within the firm and outside it. Fourth, they will be global citizens, that is, people with an open mind who are able to work across cultures as well as with NGOs, companies and governments alike. Finally, they will be able to anticipate the future. This last dimension or competency is critical to ensuring the agility that firms will require to be able to adapt quickly in a context shaped by frequent change and turmoil.

It is clear that competencies will change as well as the way those competencies have to be developed. While, as discussed above, different authors have different ideas of what these future competencies will be exactly, here I propose a framework in which different dimensions of these competencies can be reflected.

As Hatum (2010) states, throughout their careers people need to improve their interpersonal, managerial and technical competencies by developing their emotional intelligence, experience and knowledge, respectively. Gen Yers bring to firms a lot of knowledge on the use of social networks and technology. However, compared with previous generations, they are less emotionally prepared, are less engaged with organizations and are not very experienced in the functional areas of their jobs.[12] Table 4.2 summarizes the future competencies discussed above, taking into consideration the model presented by Hatum (2010).

The future leader will need to share ideas, time and decision-making. He or she will be used to delegating and happy with taking the risk that this implies. This collaborative leader will be great at helping others develop their skills, providing the right feedback and mentoring when necessary.

He or she is going to be global in all senses of the word. Global knowledge and a global mind-set will be a requirement for those

Table 4.2 *Future leadership competencies*

Dimension	Competencies of future managers
Interpersonal skills (emotional intelligence required)	Collaborative mind-set and attitude Shared leadership
Managerial skills (experience required)	Global mind-set and experience Global leadership and vision Cross-cultural interaction and knowledge
Technical skills (knowledge required)	Technologically savvy/digitally confident

working in agile and virtual firms in which global and virtual teams will perform the day-to-day operations. Dealing with people from other countries in a virtual way will make it necessary to hone their cultural knowledge and experience to be able to interact effectively.

Finally, as stated by many authors, technological knowledge and confidence will be a must to share ideas, develop projects and enhance organizational possibilities.

How can companies start to develop those skills required for future leadership? One company that has been working on developing its young workforce with the idea of creating future leaders is Rabobank Group. Rabobank is an international financial services provider founded on the basis of cooperative banking in the Netherlands and which primarily serves the food and agribusiness sector. The company has approximately 59,400 employees who serve roughly 10 million customers in 48 countries.[13] Arriving at the bank's offices, one finds an open workplace complete with art exhibits, a place where employees do not have an office but rather work anytime, anyplace. The environment is inviting and offers amenities such as cafeterias and a bakery, for example. It is a place in which one can hardly say whether the person sitting beside them is a director or an apprentice.

Ellen Koning, talent manager for ICT (Information and Communications Technology), is in charge of the Management Trainee Program that she designed. The program, which aims to integrate into the corporation the young workforce that will be the future leaders of the firm, takes into account both the characteristics of the new generation and the likely challenges that future leaders will face.

The Management Trainee Program is a two-year program in which participants build and create their own opportunities within the bank. Over the course of the program, participants have to complete three different assignments. "The first assignment is given by us, but the second and the third they look for themselves; they make a proposal to the steering committee and if it fits we agree."[14] Among the possible assignments they can work on are activities related to the bank's corporate social responsibility initiatives, such as helping Indian farmers.

Trainees not only have the opportunity to shape their assignments, but they are also provided a budget for personal development over the two years of the trainee program. The trainees can decide for themselves which courses or other training they need individually or as a group.

> We figure that not everybody needs the same things, not only on the personal development level but on the knowledge level as well. For instance, if they want as a group to be trained on personal branding, they ask me about some suppliers, I give them some names, they decide what they prefer and write a proposal to the steering committee saying, "this is what we would like to do, these are the reasons why we think we really need this, and these are the costs." So we make them responsible as a group and individually.[15]

The company has learned a lot about Gen Yers through the trainee program. As Ellen Koning points out, "They [Gen Yers] think differently; they are not bound by bad experiences in the past; they bring a lot of energy. They also work a lot more together, and they feel that sharing information boosts their work."[16]

In a nutshell, the Management Trainee Program aims to develop future managers, and this is why the new young employees are given so much freedom during the program. "We want them [trainees] to become future managers. If we teach them to only walk the line, how can they be good managers? We don't want them to be confined to this one thing; we want them to explore themselves and find out what they are good at, and hopefully they'll find it here."[17]

Rabobank's program is an example of how firms are adapting their practices and HR processes to the new generation. But what activities are most likely to develop the new generation? Taking into account what has been said before in terms of this generation's distinct set of skills but the need to develop technical, emotional and managerial competencies, a new set of activities should be designed to help this generation thrive as future leaders.

New Learning Paradigms

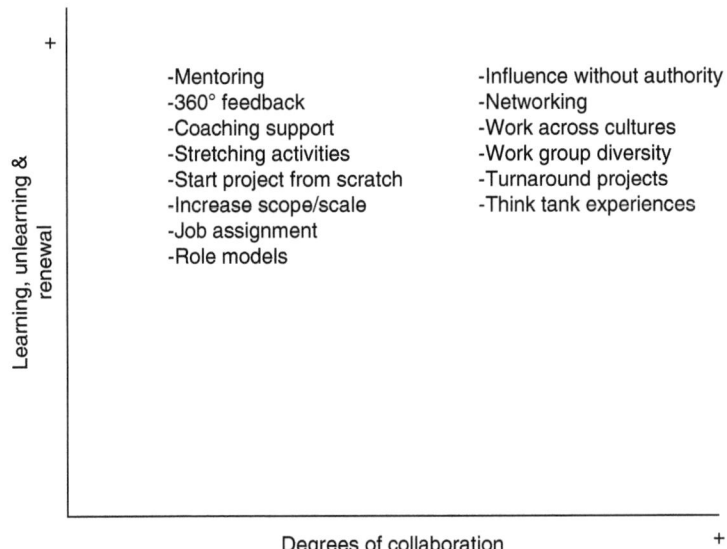

Figure 4.4 *Development activities according to their learning and collaboration impact*

To ensure the effectiveness of the development process, both the learning perspective of Gen Yers and their preference for collaboration should be taken in mind in creating development activities for them. In so doing, Gen Yers might engage in the development program and participate actively in it.

Using Figure 4.4, each company can locate the different activities in different parts of the matrix depending on the real impact of the activity for the firm. Maybe a stretching activity has a real impact on collaboration because the young employee has to not only deal with a new and tough business situation but also interact with new and different people.

Another way organizations can analyze the real impact of the different development activities is to imagine a matrix in which experience and emotional intelligence are the axes and drivers for selecting the activities that most favor those drivers (see Figure 4.5). In doing so, organizations can ensure that both managerial and interpersonal competencies can be developed.

Sujansky and Ferri-Reed (2009), for example, suggest that companies should give Millennials the broadest possible exposure

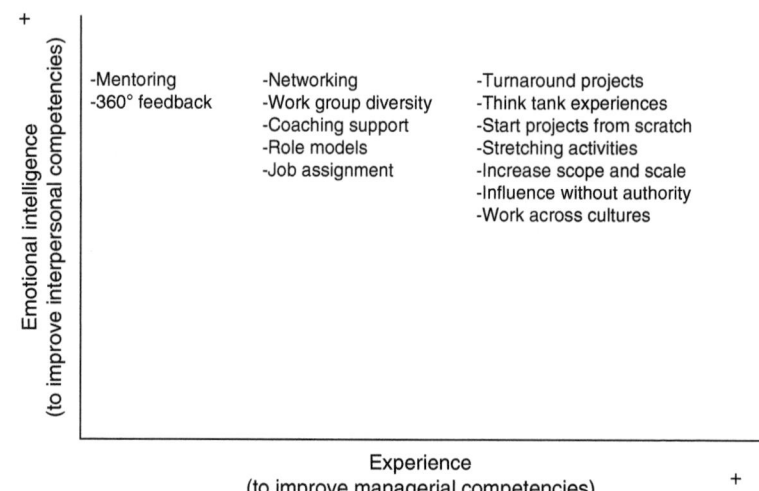

Figure 4.5 *Developing managerial and interpersonal competencies*

to the organization. Cross-training is one way to do so. Assigning new employees transitional mentors to help them to learn the ropes of the organization is another. Indeed, according to many authors, mentoring is an appropriate way to educate Millennials about how to interact with senior management. Mentoring can also help Millennials benefit from knowledge transfer and forge connections with other generations in the workplace (Magnuson and Alexander, 2008).

Other authors, such as Hatum (2010), Fulmer and Bleak (2008) and Becker et al. (1997), establish the need to balance out the different development dimensions (i.e., knowledge, experience and emotional intelligence). According to this argument, activities for developing those dimensions should be selected based on what a company wants to achieve and when. A variety of activities are needed to ensure that this multitasking generation can get the skills needed to lead in the future. Furthermore, firms' development plans need to acknowledge Gen Y's sense of urgency, developing challenging incentive programs that provide a vehicle for talented Millennial employees to grow quickly within the organization.

Recent research on developing Chinese and Indian leaders reveals the importance of the different development dimensions and activities previously analyzed. In China, for example, challenging assignments at work are the most significant stimuli for leadership development. In total, 82% of the interviewees cited challenging assignments as having a lasting impact on development, while 15% cited coursework and training as a source of leadership learning. Mistakes and failures have also been found as key drivers for leadership development. These hardship events have led to important learning. Finally, the leadership lessons on management values and communication are critical.[18]

In India, similarly to China, leadership is learned from job experiences and not in classrooms, and the events during the manager's work life from which leadership is typically learned include challenging assignments, inspiring bosses and adverse situations. Managing and motivating subordinates is also an important development experience. Positive role models and bosses who are coaches are highly valued in India's management development. For Indian managers, it is not about running the business but about leading other people and leading oneself that provide them with the critical strength to be able to succeed in running a business.[19]

While transforming systems and practices in an effort to adapt the firm to the needs and interests of the new generation has been the main focus of firms so far, the next challenge will be to ensure the current managers can lead this new generation with its different mind-set and ways of problem-solving. Martin (2005) argues that many managers misread the independent spirit of Gen Y as reluctance to conform. However, this generation does want, and need, clear direction and management support while at the same time seeking flexibility and autonomy in how it achieves its tasks and leveraging its real advantage in terms of being technologically highly literate.

Espinoza et al. (2010), in their research on managing the Millennial generation, state that effective managers of this new generation of workers have to allow their subordinates to challenge them and should use the power of their relationship rather than the power of their position. Adapting, communicating and envisioning will be key competencies of managers who want to survive the challenges posed by the new generation. By adapting, Espinoza et al. (2010) refer to the willingness to accept that a Millennial employee does not have the same experiences and values; by communicating, the authors refer to the ability to make a connection at a relational level; and by envisioning, the authors refer to lifting the horizons of those young employees who are less motivated.

Taking into account the organizational changes that will make firms more agile and virtual over time as well as the features of future leaders (learning, unlearning, renewal and collaboration) that will become more important, today's managers who face the challenge of managing and developing future leaders will need to start acquiring some competencies that relate to those skills. What are the main competencies managers should develop? Table 4.3 outlines the most relevant ones.

Adapting the leadership model is a must for companies to be able to support their managers' efforts to lead not only the new generation at work but also the transition in which overlapping generations share both workspace and leadership space. And if we also take into account the changes that organizations are going through, managers and organizations alike have great challenges ahead.

A number of companies are rethinking their leadership framework to enhance the likelihood of managers' success. One example is Pernod Ricard, a large international wine and spirit producer with net sales in 2011 of €7.6 billion, 18,000 employees in 70 countries and 17 brands among the world's top 100.[20] Pernod Ricard has increased its market share in recent years through both organic growth and acquisitions of companies such as Seagrams (2001) and Allied Domecq (2005). Absolut, Chivas, Mumm and Beefeater are among the famous brands in the company's portfolio.

Flexibility is a key value that the company has always tried to preserve. Thus, for instance, Pernod Ricard has a decentralized structure in which brand companies and market companies interact with each other. The idea behind this structure is in line with the concept "think globally, act locally." More recently,

Table 4.3 *Managerial competencies and Millennials' characteristics*

Millennials' characteristics	Managerial competencies required
Work-life integration	• *Allowing* the new generation to integrate its work life and personal life • *Engaging* the young workforce in their jobs and the organization by making sure the space and attitude are provided for employees to release their imagination and enjoy their jobs • *Rewarding and recognizing* a job well done • *Providing* opportunities for knowledge sharing and transfer • *Teaching* the limits between organizational life and personal life, helping employees connect the big picture and the operational implications of their ideas • *Communicating* clearly expectations, results and feedback
Multitasking	• *Connecting* the Millennials to their tasks and projects • *Supporting* the performance of the young workforce by helping them focus • *Listening* to the ideas of Millennials who have an open mind and a different view regarding what should be done and how • *Forming* team-based projects to boost the performance of a generation used to teamwork
Tech savvy	• *Allowing* Millennials to access their favorite technologies in the workplace to help them find inspiration for and challenge in their jobs • *Adopting* Millennials' ideas that come from their technological knowledge
Social awareness	• *Inspiring* people through their example of moral behavior and justice at work • *Getting involved* in social initiatives both outside and within the organization

the company has created what it calls an "agility project" that aims to speed up the response of the company to market changes while making the company more responsive and adaptable as well.

"Agility is our driver of change. Companies need to be agile to adapt fast to the environment,"[21] states Jaime Jordana, global corporate director of HR development at Pernod. This agile firm incorporates the new workforce, which it views as the force of change and company growth: "The new generation inquires about our culture, our results, where it will work, about flexible jobs and our corporate social responsibility, taking into account the impact of alcohol on people."[22]

Adaptability and agility require a different approach toward leadership. As such, Pernod Ricard reframed its leadership model to incorporate a set of competencies designed to enhance managers' ability to succeed in terms of leading the transition toward a more agile firm. Strategic visioning, entrepreneurship, results orientation and values-driven decision-making are accompanied by two competencies that focus on people and are critical for the way the young generation needs to be led: people development and team management. "We want, on the one hand, leaders who are able to differentiate themselves as capable of transforming teams into high-performing teams and, on the other hand, leaders who are able to get to know people, the people who work with them and will be the future leaders."[23] To support the new competencies scheme, the firm created a new tool called "I Lead" to help managers relate to the new generation. With "I Lead," managers can assess leadership factors, leadership styles and performance, allowing them to deepen their conversations with their young and bright employees in terms of "understanding what they want to do, how they want to approach it and the ability of the company to accomplish this. So with 'I Lead' we are determined to make sure that managers and Millennials can find a common ground of understanding."[24]

The challenge that organizations have to confront is twofold: develop future leaders so that they can succeed in their future careers and in running the organization, and develop current leaders to be able to champion firms through the difficult transition they need to go through until Millennials are ready to take over the most important positions in the companies. At the same time, Gen Yers will have a series of difficult decisions to make in their race to leadership positions. Hurdles need to be avoided or jumped over throughout their careers. Those careers will be different and as such companies will need to transform their systems as well as practices to adapt to the new generation and thereby ensure Millennials are willing to commit to and develop in the companies. In the next section, we delve into the new career paradigms for future generations.

Future Trends: Learning through Technology[25]

> Exposure to digital technology is changing the way people think, changing cognitive patterns, creating a whole new set of perceptions about the world. The basic difference with the people who come new into the workforce is that they know about technology first and have seen the technology in their lives before they come to work. They look at the workplace and say, "How can I use these tools and technologies that I know?" Facebook, mobile computing and emergent kinds of collaboration such as wikis have been successful strategies for them as students, citizens and consumers. So they ask themselves, "How can I bring that into the workplace, how can I adapt this technology to existing business practices, how do I bring a social network into an existing process?" so it is a different thought pattern in the workplace.
>
> A lot of established businesses are really struggling to communicate effectively with customers using social media – not the technology, which is trivial, but the whole mind-set that comes with it. They are only now waking up to the idea that transparency, sincerity and social responsibility are real and important to their customers. The Millennial generation has been marinated in digital culture from an early age. They get it. The businesses they start do not have

to reinvest in new technology or a new culture to operate effectively in this environment.

Older firms are organized as a centralized hierarchy because, before these new technologies, that was the most efficient way to distribute information: people at the top making decisions, down through the layers to the people executing those decisions. That was efficient, that was good for Industrial Age organizations. But if suddenly I can text messages to the CEO or be friends on Facebook or whatever, and it removes these channels, or you have somebody in one subsidiary that you can collaborate with across boundaries, then you have two different modes of organization clashing. An older person wouldn't even think of suggesting such collaboration due to the mind-set that "this person's in a different part of the organization, I am not going to bother them." The social convention for people that predated the new technology makes it hard for them to use it naturally in the same way that a younger person would.

When you bring in a new technology, it's going to disrupt older ways of working, so you need to tell your older workers who have the knowledge to run the business that it's OK to share and participate. And that's not always a conversation! The IT department is not prepared to have that conversation.

Organizations require developing people through mentoring. It usually goes from the more experienced business person to the less experienced person coming into the business. Now, however, sometimes it is the case that the less experienced people coming into the firm know more about the technology and, in a private environment, can help the executives of the company understand how to use the technology better. And, at the same time, the older executive is imparting the wisdom of the business and knowledge of it to the young people. So there is a two-way dialog that forms the basis of a great relationship.

> **Ideas at a Glance**
>
> **Developing the Future Leaders**
>
> - Development plans for Gen Yers will need to take into consideration collaboration and learning opportunities, on the one hand, and unlearning and renewal opportunities, on the other.
> - Future leaders will still need to develop interpersonal, managerial and technical competencies. The difference will be in the competencies required for leading in the future and the mix of activities required to grow and advance.
> - Current managers will need to develop competencies that help them understand Millennials' characteristics and develop Millennials into future leaders, and thereby help create a more agile and virtual firm.

TOPSY TURVY: CAREERS RELOADED

One may guess that the transformation organizations will go through over time, the agility and virtuality that are shaping firms and the changes associated with the new generation entering the workforce will determine what careers will look like in the future.

While on average career paths seemed stable only a few years ago, the changes the new generation is imposing on the market make the future of careers rife with uncertainty. Gen Yers, by nature, are likely to change jobs more frequently as they seek the best career path along which they can integrate their personal and professional objectives. While the market presented no evidence of a dramatic change in job security over the 1990s (Schmidt and Svorny, 1998), a study by Farber (2008) on job tenure between 1973 and 2006 shows that employees are less likely to have a long-term position in companies, as evidenced by sharp declines in tenure. Farber (2008) shows further that over the period he analyzed there has been a steady increase in "churn," that is, the proportion of workers with less than one year of tenure in their jobs. However, the decline in tenure has been less pronounced among women.

Things that were previously considered futuristic are now becoming real in the fast-changing and more virtual firm. In particular, as the workplace is being reconfigured so as to cater to and incorporate the young workforce, we are seeing a more open, flexible and adjustable work environment with employees less tied to traditional offices and timetables. Elements of the virtual firm are starting to emerge, such as videoconferencing, digital signage and the fast evolution of virtual networks.

The jobs themselves are also being redesigned. Work has become more dynamic. Rigid job descriptions are being replaced by competency-based job definitions and team-based control over projects.

In Chapter 1, we analyzed the different ways of organizing that are shaping the ways organizations restructure themselves. Organizational structures are already flatter and challenging the traditional hierarchical-based career progression. As an example of the remarkable shift in the way firms are structuring themselves, Benko and Anderson (2010) report the following data: In the 1980s General Electric accounted for 17 layers; whereas by the mid-1990s it had only seven layers. Furthermore, the number of management levels between division heads and the CEO has declined 25%.

Given the foregoing, one might ask how careers will be affected by all these changes. How will Millennials be tempted to stay with a company if they are likely to want to change jobs all the time. The answer is that careers will have different paradigm, what we call here "career reloaded."

Many theories and ideas exist about the shape new careers will take. While some of these ideas have been put into practice, there are some important conceptual developments we need to tackle to be able to understand the shifts in careers, what the future trends are and where the main challenges will be.

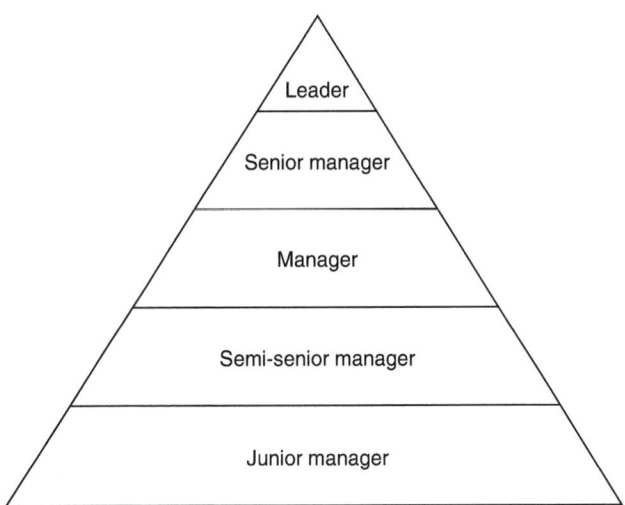

Figure 4.6 *An example of a career ladder*

One important theoretical and practical development has been the idea of replacing the traditional career ladder with a career lattice. According to Benko and Anderson (2010), a career ladder refers to a linear climb to the top, while a career lattice refers to the possibility of a multidirectional path with moves across, up and down the organizational structure. Figure 4.6 and Table 4.4 provide examples of a career ladder and career lattice.

Benko and Anderson (2010) suggest that careers paths no longer involve climbing straight up the corporate ladder but rather pursuing a series of climbs, lateral moves and planned descents along the corporate lattice. The shift toward lattice thinking represents a paradigm shift in terms of career development. Instead of providing lifetime employment (something that in today's context Millennials might be reluctant to accept and firms might be reluctant to offer), lattice organizations become "career enhancers," making sure that employees gain the skills they need at each stage of their careers. No more "career advancement" per se. Rather, as the authors put it, "the more skills and experience people gain, the more likely they are to stay with an employer" (Benko and Anderson, 2010: 11).

Table 4.4 *An example of a career lattice*

Area 1	Area B	Area C	Area D
Leader	Leader	Leader	Leader
Senior manager	Senior manager	Senior manager	Senior manager
Manager	Manager	Manager	Manager
Senior manager	Senior manager	Senior manager	Senior manager
Semi-senior manager	Semi-senior manager	Semi-senior manager	Semi-senior manager
Junior manager	Junior manager	Junior manager	Junior manager

Based on the model of Benko and Anderson (2010).

This idea is emphasized by Penelope Trunk, founder of Gen Y online community Brazen Careerist, who says that "the only reason a Gen Yer job hops is to keep their learning curve high.... Gen Y knows that there are no lifetime jobs anymore."[26] Hatum (2010) also points out that employability instead of employment is what keeps Millennials motivated and gives organizations the opportunity to retain them longer.

The concept of a career lattice is not new. Arthur and Rousseau (1996) introduce the concept of a boundaryless career compared with a bounded organizational career. The latter is "bounded" within the organization and might be similar to the career ladder. The former, in contrast, does not have a single form, but instead may take different possible forms. Bounded careers include concepts such as job grades, promotions, demotions, plateauing and fast-tracking. Boundaryless careers maintain the perspective that people take responsibility for their own career path and include concepts such as networks, knowledge and self-management.

In the early 1990s, British management guru Charles Handy (1989, 1994) predicted that the idea of pursuing one full-time job would be replaced with the idea of working on several different part-time jobs. He called this the "portfolio career," where portfolio work comprises packages of work arrangements for the plying and selling of an individual's skills in a variety of contexts.

The demise of the traditional, hierarchical career has also been widely predicted, as has been its replacement by the proliferation of more fluid and individual career choices (Mallon, 1998). While the career lattice appears to well capture current career trajectories and some people might be tempted to pursue a portfolio career, Gratton (2011) firmly acknowledges the importance of becoming a "serial master" to add real value. For young professionals, this might mean a fundamental shift from being "a shallow generalist" who knows a little about a lot to being a master with in-depth knowledge and competencies in a number of different domains (Gratton, 2011: e-book location 3010). A serial master demonstrates deep knowledge and skills in a particular area, creating networks that tap into others' deep knowledge. Gratton's career concept is rooted in resource-based theory that states that competitive advantages are only possible with resources (i.e., competencies in Gratton's career definition) that are valuable, rare and hard to imitate.

We have so far discussed many concepts, some of which are at odds or at least appear to be at odds. So how does this help us understand how organizations can cope with the flattening of their structures and the need for Millennials' career enhancement? How can Millennials follow a lattice career path that allows them to acquire expertize while developing across the organization? Table 4.5 is an attempt to link and summarize Millennials' characteristics, careers and organizations.

Millennials will make sure that their careers do not outshine their personal life. In an attempt to protect the life they want to have, Millennials may prefer to decelerate the pace of their career progression or reduce their workload and responsibilities. For them, there will always be a chance to get back to work after they find equilibrium between their professional and personal lives. The organizational challenge is to start coming up with career paths that meet both employees' and the organization's needs. Career customization will move companies away from the "one-size-fits-all" notion of career progression toward multiple career paths in which personalized paths meet individuals' interests.

Table 4.5 *Millennials' characteristics and implications for careers and organizations*

Millennials' characteristics	Career implications	Organizational implications
Work-life integration	• If the career does not lead to work-life balance, the individual might try to find another career option • Employees want to work like at home • Career pace, responsibilities and roles will depend on one's personal aims and life objectives	• Tailor career paths to the individual • Adapt work infrastructure to cater to employees' needs • Align HR practices with changing careers
Multitasking	• Job hopping will occur if learning needs are not satisfied • Job hopping will occur as a way to gain knowledge and expertize	• Accelerate internal mobility • Support career enhancement instead of career advancement to provide learning opportunities within the firm and retain people
Tech savvy	• Technology and social networks will be used to expand one's career possibilities • Learning will be supported by technology and networks	• Allow access to and invest in technology • Support social networking to enhance learning opportunities

(*continued*)

Table 4.5 *Continued*

Millennials' characteristics	Career implications	Organizational implications
		• Trust employees' technological expertize to leverage problem-solving potential for firm
Social awareness	• Career expertize will not be detached from values and beliefs	• Update mission statement to make sure firm values are aligned with Millennials' social awareness and sense of social responsibility

In an attempt to meet people's needs to customize their careers, and hence in an effort to retain talent, firms have been implementing flexible work arrangements that foster a more open environment. There are many forms of flexible work. Dychtwald et al. (2006) suggest that some of the basic options include flexible time (i.e., flexible hours and shifts, compressed workweeks etc.), reduced time (i.e., part-time and seasonal work, reduced hours or the number of workdays) and flexible place (i.e., telecommuting, mobile work and other ways of working on an offsite basis).

Many firms have started to implement such systems. As an example, 70% of employees at Cisco Systems now regularly work from home at least 20% of the time. Similarly, 34% of the employees at Booz Allen Hamilton and 32% of the employees at SC Johnson & Sons work from home at least 20% of the time.[27]

As another example, JetBlue, which has worked to ingrain flexibility into its culture, now has its entire customer support team working from home.[28] And Best Buy's Results-Only Work Environment (ROWE) program allows employees in participating departments to work virtually anywhere, anytime as long as they successfully complete their assignments on time. This shift has resulted in an increase in productivity of 41% and a decrease in employee turnover of as much as 90% at headquarters (Ferriss, 2009).

Even Wall Street has started to adapt to the flex culture. At investment consulting firm Accordion Partners,[29] two ex-university colleagues hired out experienced investment bankers by the hour. One might think that any banker with a decent resume would be hesitant to gamble his or her career on a company like this. However, Accordion has no shortage of clients, and the firm has been flooded with resumes from proven professionals eager to give up to 80-hour weeks for the chance to control their own schedules.[30]

Nick Leopard, founder and co-owner of Accordion decided to set up this venture after the birth of his son. "Banking life means that your life is not yours anymore. I remember Saturday nights with my wife at the movies, and I had to leave in the middle of the performance. So, with my partner, we started to think about how to offer clients and employees options that they never had before. Our challenge was to change the way we work in finance."[31]

Professionals at Accordion pick up their assignments, work from wherever they prefer and observe an informal dress code. The aim of these practices was clear to Leopard: "Why not make people happy while they are working? Our employees joined us for various reasons. Maybe they want to start a family and devote time to them, or they are starting an entrepreneurial endeavor and they need flexibility."[32] At Accordion, people can choose their assignments and establish their schedules. "They can be very busy for two months working 80 hours a week, but later come back and say, 'Nick, for the next two months I will be surfing in Hawaii, put me back on track after this break'."[33]

The system allows people to pursue their own business ventures as well. "We have a bright analyst, our clients love her. She set up a photograph business. With our different way of thinking about work, she can have her own business as well, something that would be impossible in a traditional bank."[34] Accordion employees do not receive bonuses like typical bankers do; instead, it sets its pay to be commensurate with what a banker would earn throughout the year if that year end-bonus were paid out over 12 months.

For Nick Leopard, the system works because people rely on the system. While "in a traditional bank you are just a number, here if you are 30 years old, you can meet the CEO of a company and help him run financial projections."[35]

Are the foregoing practices sufficient to meet the career customization and enhancement needs of Millennials? It seems not because problems continue to emerge. Why? Because while people feel that flexible work arrangements are useful in managing and planning their personal lives, such arrangements also limit their career prospects. Employees fear that organizations might offer these systems of flexibility but at the same time view those who enroll in these programs as uncommitted. Questions that employees ask themselves include "What the career consequences are of joining a flexible arrangement? Am I putting my career at risk? Will my job be in jeopardy?" Thus, there remain concerns involved with taking advantage of flexible work systems.

In essence, the main issue with flexible work systems is that they do not address people's need to build careers via paths other than the one offered by a career ladder. People's priorities are changing and yet companies are still promoting rigid career paths that offer career advancement in the traditional fashion.

Is there a different perspective that can help organizations sort out this problem? Benko and Weisberg (2007) call this necessity of customizing careers *mass career customization* (MCC). MCC assumes a set of options along four career dimensions: pace, workload, location/schedule and role. Pace refers to how quickly an employee can accept increased responsibility, workload refers to the amount of work a person can handle over time, location/schedule refers to where work is performed or when work gets done and role refers to the employee's position and responsibility. According to the authors, the four dimensions of MCC may vary over time according to people's needs. For example, an employee can increase or decrease the pace of the job, can have a full or reduced workload, can have restricted or complete mobility and can serve in a line or staff capacity or be considered an individual contributor or leader. The exact combination of these dimensions depends on people's choices and the organization's needs.

I propose a perspective in which organizations adapt and customize careers as a way to satisfy Millennials' need to develop their own portfolio careers and at the same time commit them to the organization. I call this perspective *customized portfolio career* (CPC). *Customized* refers to employees being able to find a fit with their need to develop particular skills, and *portfolio career* refers to employees being able to move across the organization acquiring knowledge and experience depending on the competencies they want to develop (and the competencies the organization expects to require of them in the future).

To better understand the idea of CPC, consider two cases. Figure 4.7 summarizes Richard's case.

Richard studied business administration and was delighted when he got a job in the commercial department of a large firm. During his fast-track career, he considered a wide variety of options to further his development. Acquiring functional experience together with people skills were necessary to become a manager, Richard's career aim. After obtaining these skills, he went back to the commercial field managing big accounts and getting acquainted with the latest trends in the field. Finally, he had the opportunity to start working in one of the firm's business units and, based on his broad knowledge and experience with the firm, he ultimately became a fine manager.

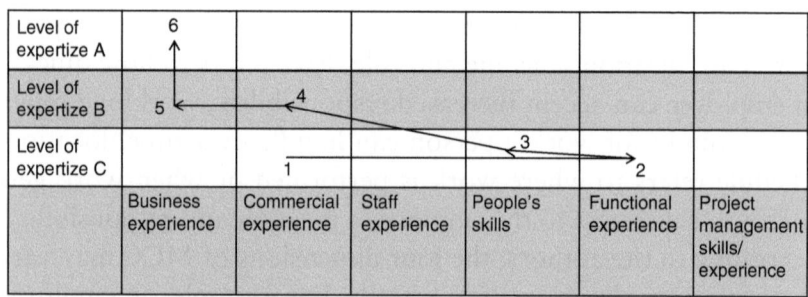

Figure 4.7 *An approach toward a customized portfolio career (CPC): Richard's case*

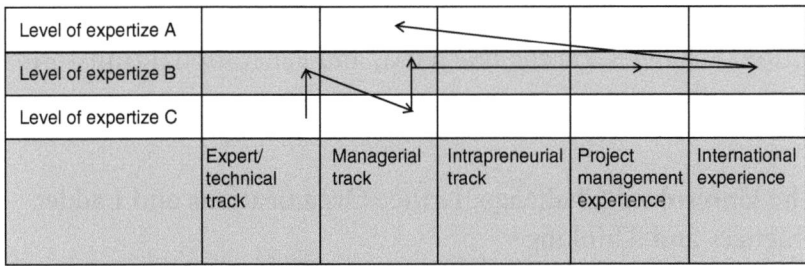

Figure 4.8 *An approach toward a CPC: Anika's case*

Figure 4.8 summarizes Anika's case.

In the case of Anika, a young technical expert at an IT firm, she showed promise and was considering a career that would lead to a management position with the firm. The company believes that a good manager needs to have project management skills and international experience. Looking forward to these challenges, Anika was offered both opportunities over the course of four years. These opportunities allowed her to consolidate her knowledge and experience. At the end of these opportunities, Anika decided to continue her managerial-track IT career to support the growth of the organization.

The CPC approach has the advantage of providing both the organization and the employee real customization. For the employee, CPC customizes one's career path in a way that enhances his or her career, as Benko and Anderson (2010) explain. For organizations, CPC allows different frameworks to be created for different units or divisions to help firms align their strategic aims with people's expectations. CPC thus supersedes more narrow approaches in which some dimensions are generalized. In particular, the CPC approach allows each business unit or area of a company to have its own unique view toward the career path of its employees.

The new career paradigm proposed in this section helps shed light on how to respond to the changes happening in the workplace as a result of the new learning style, development needs and attitude of the young generation entering the workforce. The reader should not see this new possible career paradigm as a mere fad, but should instead integrate it along with the organizational changes, on the one hand, and generational transformation, on the other.

The Unresolved Challenge: Lattice Organizations and Ladder Practices and Thinking

> Companies are trying to become more agile, and as a result lattice organizational forms, as Benko and Anderson (2010) suggest, are starting to emerge everywhere. Lattice organizational structures are a way to quickly adapt to an ever-changing context. However, companies still rely on HR practices rooted in a ladder way of thinking.
>
> The shift from corporate ladder to lattice requires not only that a firm update its mental models to a new reality of working but also adapt its ways of thinking about careers and HR practices so that they fit into the new reality.
>
> Today's flatter organizations provide fewer opportunities to move people up the ladder. Yet while lattice organizations are broadening employees' development possibilities, how the work is done and some HR practices are still part of the old ladder culture of working. For instance, while firms are transforming into increasingly virtual workplaces, some companies still require that employees have a full-time physical presence. Similarly, while the lattice idea of organization functions as a way to increase collaboration beyond the organizational level, some companies still use hierarchical and functional structures that work against a more dynamic way of organizing.
>
> Some HR practices have also been influenced by the notion that career paths are linked to compensation. We do not fault HR departments for subscribing to this view – it works perfectly well in a context of career ladder thinking: the higher you are in the structure, the higher your salary will be. Besides, if you are on a managerial track, the chances

of earning more money are higher over time. The consequences of this view? Strong technical people, experts and critical talent moving into the ranks of upper management to be able to get a better compensation deal. And the result? Unhappiness and frustration.

Some firms are aware of the importance of adapting and aligning career paths with a more agile organization. Lockheed Martin Company, for example, lists current projects of interest to key technical talent to harness a sense of purpose and align individual goals with organizational projects. At Genetech, the company identifies 16 scientific options that are possible to explore within the organization so that prospective candidates can appreciate the breadth of career choices available to them. These companies are focusing their efforts on attracting and retaining experts, making sure they will be able to succeed in a dynamic, lattice-based organization.[36]

Current HR practices in many firms still imply that you should move up in the ladder in order to get an increase in compensation. Forming a lattice organization, for many firms still an aim to be achieved, will require an assessment of HR practices so that they can start to reward lattice careers as well.

Ideas at a Glance

Careers Upside Down

- A career ladder refers to a linear climb to the top, a concept with origins in industrial organizations.

- A career lattice refers to a multidimensional path across, up and down the organizational structure as one's career progresses.

- A boundaryless career and a portfolio career are among the new concepts recently introduced to describe the new types of career paths adopted by people and organizations.

- A CPC (Customized Portfolio Career), involves adapting and customizing careers to satisfy the needs of the new generation at work while also satisfying the needs of the organization.

Questions for Managers

- What is your organization doing to adapt to Millennials' different ways of learning?

- What is your organizational learning strategy?

    o Is it based on individual learning? formal learning? experiential learning? collaborative learning?

- What are the new competencies your organization is defining for future leaders?

    o Has your firm thought about the differences between current and future leaders?

    o Has your firm thought about the transition between current and future leadership and the competencies required to go through such a process?

- What are the activities your company is expected to implement to accelerate leadership development among the younger employees?

    o Do those activities take into account the importance and impact of collaboration and learning?

- What are the main competencies current managers should develop to make sure they can lead the generational transition as well as the transition toward a more agile and virtual firm?
- How is your organization managing the flattening of organizational structures and the need for career enhancement and employability?

CASE IN POINT: LA MASÍA–BARCELONA CLUB – A TALENT DEVELOPMENT SCHOOL FOR THE FUTURE

From left to right: FC Barcelona shield; Camp Nou, the stadium of the Barcelona Club; La Masía, the Club's youth academy for talent development. Pictures courtesy of FC Barcelona.

Founded in 1899 by a group of young foreigners living in Barcelona, FC Barcelona was the result of the increasing popularity of football as well as other British sports. Since 2004, the Barça (as the Club is called) has won the UEFA Champions League, the greatest contest in professional football, three times. It has also won La Liga, Spain's domestic league, five times; claimed two UEFA Super Cup titles; and two FIFA Club World Cup titles, among the most important of its achievements. A recent article suggested that the Club has a constellation of top talent: Eight members of the Spanish national football team that won the 2010 FIFA World Cup in South Africa play for Barça.[37]

The greatest international recognition came when in 2010 FIFA Ballon D'Or nominations short-listed Xavi, Iniesta and Messi for the honor, all three of whom had grown up at La Masía, FC Barcelona's youth academy, a residence where 75 young athletes of 12 to 17 years old are trained and educated at a state-of-the-art facility.[38] Taking a long-term strategy, FC Barcelona opened La Masía in 1979 with the idea of developing its own players, groomed and brought up at home. La Masía has become the pillar of the Club's current success.

Jordi Mestre, one of the directors on the Club's board and individually responsible for the formation and development of "Fútbol Base" (initial football), explains,

> Strategically, La Masía is a competitive advantage because when kids reach the top team, they adapt very fast. Other teams that would like to reach this level have to be patient and need to know that the work they are doing today will be seen by other generations. You need to work for the Club, and in our football world this is difficult because you want results. A new manager always wants to see quick results. They do not have the patience to wait and bet on young people developing in places such as La Masía. Well, we do that.[39]

So how is the Club dealing with the challenges posed by its Gen Yers and even younger generations? What development framework does it use to make sure that learning efficiency is achieved? Is intuition or evolution the way to produce a good player? La Masía employs the Club's method for developing young people and in particular good players. This method consists of four pillars: talent, physical condition, personality and context.

Talent is what the Club's scouts look for in the market. Scouts tour the whole country for children and beyond the Spanish borders for adults. Next, while physical strength may be sought after by scouts in sports such as basketball, Carles Folguera, La Masía's director, emphasizes that "[a]t La Masía, physical condition is more relevant than physical strength. We look after how to take care of children's bodies . . . through what we eat, how we sleep etc."[40]

Personality is the third pillar of the development program at La Masía because the youngsters' attitudes and effort all count toward their development. The director of La Masía is clear regarding the importance of personality: "If to one's talent we add humbleness and effort, you can have great talent. Talent alone is not enough . . . you find kids with great personalities and leadership skills that prepare them to have a good career." Guillermo Amor, director of football training and an ex-professional football player who was one of the first residents at La Masía in 1979, explains further: "Effort is a part of the personality of those who want to reach a place here and stay for the long term. We insist on the value of studying and working hard. We make sure kids realize how difficult it is to reach the top."[41]

The fourth pillar of the development program at La Masía is context. La Masía influences kids in the day-to-day: "We are mothers and fathers," emphasizes Carles Folguera, "We see the kids everyday, how they perform at school, how they behave, if one is a positive leader, if he gets involved, if he gets obsessed."[42]

Among the four pillars of development, Folguera stresses that personality, context and talent are the most critical:

> In football, the physical aspects are not so critical in our model. Here we have Messi, Iniesta, Xavi, Alves . . . all players with normal or small bodies. However, we relied on their talent and helped them develop other resources and competencies, such as intelligence, knowledge about the technical aspects of the game, decision-making ability etc. Do you think these players I mentioned before would have been selected as potential professional football players in the United Kingdom when they were kids? . . . I do not think so; they were too small for their standards![43]

With just one and a half hours of training each day, the focus at La Masía is on developing the future players' understanding of the technical and methodological aspects of the game, instilling

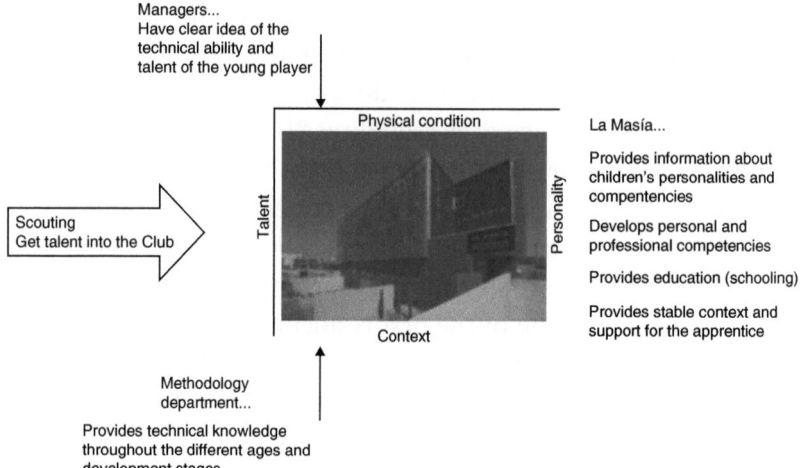

Figure 4.9 *An integrated process: Developing talent at FC Barcelona*

in the children the Club's values, developing nonsports competencies that will affect the youths' future abilities and generating committed future players (See Figure 4.9).

In sum, intuition is not sufficient to identify future talent or to assure that a person who shows potential will reach the top team at the Club. As Guillermo Amor remarked, "You need to develop people, and developing people requires time. You also need to make sure you are well focused on the development process, thinking always about the long term."[44] La Masía provides some empirical support for the presumption that performance differences between individuals could be explained by time spent training (Farrow, 2012). Without significant investment in practice, such as the case of future players at the Barcelona Club, sufficient skill acquisition to become an expert player and excel in the field would be unlikely.

5
The New Realignment Contract

IN SEARCH OF . . . AGILITY

Management theorists and practitioners alike are always trying to find the best ways for organizations to be effective, adaptable and, most importantly, successful. When introduced in the late 1970s, the 7-S framework was a watershed in thinking about organizational effectiveness. Previously, the focus of managers was on organizational structure – who does what, who reports to whom and the like. "Does strategy follow structure or the other way around?" was the question of the day. As organizations grew in size and complexity, however, the focus shifted to problems related to coordination.

Featured in the article "Structure is not Organization" (1980), and later in the best selling book *In Search of Excellence* by former McKinsey consultants Thomas J. Peters and Robert H. Waterman (1982), the 7-S framework maps a constellation of interrelated factors that influence an organization's ability to adapt and change. The lack of hierarchy among these factors suggests that significant progress in one part of the organization would be difficult without progress in the others. While hierarchy is absent, "hard" factors (i.e., structure, strategy and systems) and "soft" factors (i.e., staff, skills, style and shared values) are easily identified. Soft factors are not easy to spot from outside the organization; deep knowledge of the real life of the firm is required.

Figure 5.1 shows the 7-S framework.

Thirty years after it was introduced, the 7-S framework remains an important framework for organizational analysis. Yet

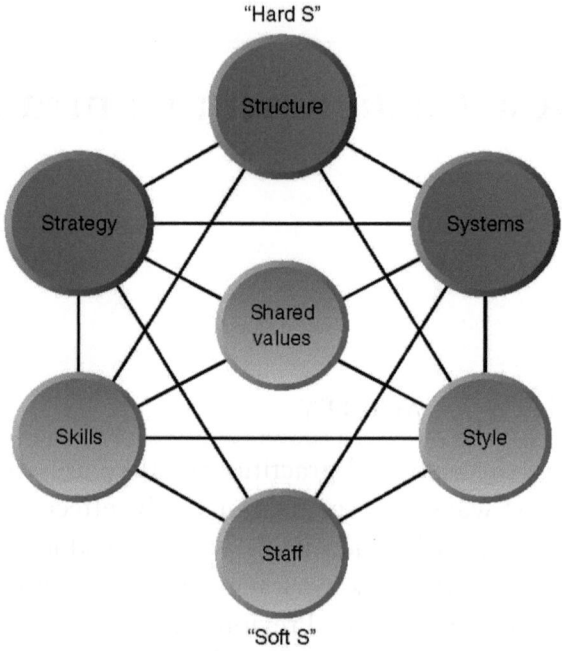

Figure 5.1 *7-S framework (based on Peters and Waterman, 1982)*

most of the firms described by Peters and Waterman as among the best-run firms have either disappeared or observed a decline in performance since the early 1970s. A new framework for understanding organizations is therefore clearly required.

Scott Keller and Colin Price, both directors at McKinsey, have recently proposed a superseding framework that, as the name of their book *Beyond Performance* suggests, is based on the idea that performance (i.e., "what the enterprise delivers to its stakeholders in financial and operational terms" (2011: 5)) is no longer enough to be effective and to build or maintain competitive advantage. According to these authors, health, which they define as the "ability of an organization to align, execute, and renew itself faster than the competition so that it can sustain exceptional performance over time" (Keller and Price, 2011: 5), is also critical. So instead of talking about 7 Ss, they propose 5 As: *aspire, assess, architect, act* and *advance*. The 5 As offer answers to questions such as where do we want to go, how ready are we, what do we need to do to get there, how do we manage the journey and how do we keep moving forward?

To achieve organizational health, firms need to have key attributes such as internal alignment, quality execution and capacity for renewal. Each attribute is complemented by various elements to make sure the organization can demonstrate good health. For instance, internal alignment is complemented by the elements direction, leadership, culture and climate; quality execution is complemented by the elements accountability, coordination, control, capabilities, leadership and motivation; and capacity for renewal is complemented by the elements external orientation, leadership, innovation and learning.

Figure 5.2 illustrates the main dimensions of Keller and Price framework.

What is clear from the above discussion is that the increase in organizational complexity is requiring a different framework of analysis. Frameworks created with the aim of achieving organizational effectiveness need to take into consideration the changes we have been analyzing throughout the book: the organizational changes that will lead to more agile and virtual firms and generational changes that will affect the way people work and how firms conceive of and structure work.

First and foremost, companies need to adapt quickly to make sure that they not only achieve greater competitive advantage but that they also actually survive. Sustainability over the long term should be a clear objective for firms.

Recall that organizational agility was defined in Chapter 1 as the ability of the organization to adapt quickly under conditions of rapid change. Agility will allow firms to quickly identify the best ways to organize, the best ways to absorb the new workforce and the best ways to leverage the workforce's competencies for the good of the company – organizational capabilities that will be necessary to confront the changes in the external environment that firms will increasingly face in the future. Not surprisingly, the concepts of *health* as defined by Keller and Price (2011)

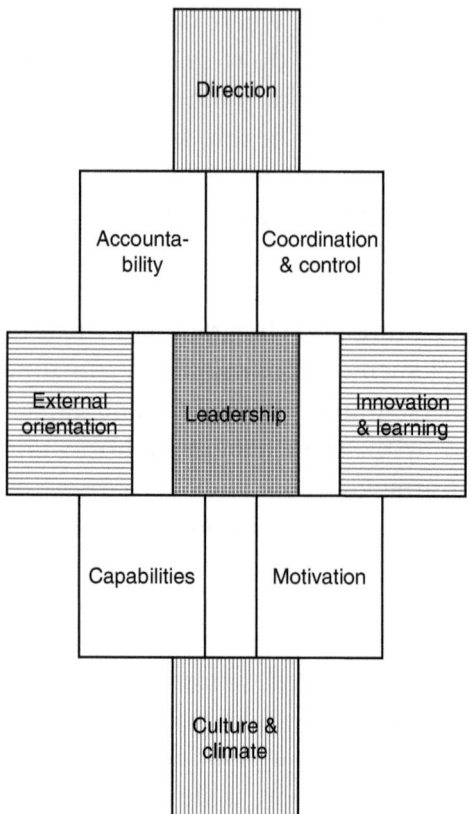

Figure 5.2 *Nine elements of organizational health (based on Keller and Price, 2011)*

and of *organizational agility* complement one another: The former stresses the importance of performance over the long term, while the latter emphasizes the importance of being able to adapt quickly to respond to external and internal changes. Underlying both of these concepts is the idea of long-run sustainability.

Achieving organizational agility will not be simple, but it can help firms ensure their future sustainability. Chapter 1 listed some indicators of what an agile firm might look like. However, how does an organization become more agile? Figure 5.3 presents a simple model of organizational agility that brings together many of the concepts discussed previously in the book.

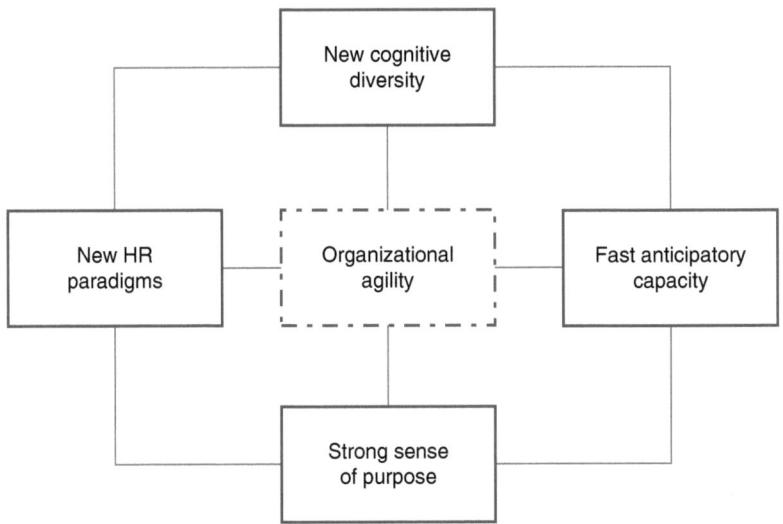

Figure 5.3 *A model of organizational agility*

New Cognitive Diversity

New cognitive diversity will be brought into organizations by the new generation entering the workforce. The rapid incorporation of Millennials into the workplace has the potential to enhance the adaptability and creativity of organizations. The diversity of skills and backgrounds as well as the introduction of fresh ideas with respect to how to manage and work will bring more heterogeneity to the fore. Diverse ideas lead to the use of a variety of information sources and perspectives, enhancing creativity and innovation in decision-making (Wiersema and Bantel, 1992). Furthermore, multiple competing views can facilitate radical change and rapid adaptation (Webb and Pettigrew, 1999).

Consistent with these arguments, Hatum (2007) states that cognitive diversity improves the capacity to act, on the one hand, and stimulates constructive conflict, on the other. The former allows organizations to respond more swiftly to market changes. The latter, while increasing disagreement, provides agile firms with more alternatives to choose from. Companies able to integrate Millennials and involve them in more critical decisions will therefore benefit from their fresh approach toward management and problem-solving.

Best Buy is one company in the United States that supports, engages with and profits from the cognitive diversity brought by Gen Yers. Being one of the most important employers of Millennials in America, the company quickly adapted and has benefited from Millennials' innovative approach toward work.

The firm has launched its own in-house social networking platform called "Blue Shirt Nation" that allows store employees to ask questions and share ideas. The idea behind this platform is to encourage a culture of innovation in which everyone can question, experiment and make mistakes. These forums feed innovation at Best Buy.[1]

In the midst of the 2008 crisis, the company relied on Net Geners' knowledge of internet technology to help the firm save money. A group of Millennial employees were put together to produce a new portal for about US$250,000, a cost that was much lower than the several million-dollar estimate provided by consultants.[2]

The cognitive diversity and fresh ideas the new generation is bringing into the workforce can make companies more innovative and in turn agile and adaptable. The fresh approach of Gen Yers may even boost the ability of firms to generate new businesses.

As Hamel (2007: 216) suggests, the real problem for an established firm is not a dearth of ideas but the fact that "management processes and practices reflexively favour 'more of the same' over 'new and different'." Lack of management diversity (i.e., homogeneity of ideas) leads to indifference to and/or skepticism about new business ideas. Millennials and future generations can thus help generate new ideas, processes and products.

Fast Anticipatory Capacity

Daft and Weick (1984) state that the capacity to interpret is a key element that distinguishes human organizations from others. To draw a deep interpretative analysis, scanning the environment is a fundamental activity.

Morrison (1992) argues that organizations need a method that allows decision-makers to first understand the external environment and the interconnections between its various sectors and then translate this understanding into the organization's planning and decision-making process.

By scanning the environment, companies can receive signals, mobilize resources and be more proactive, creating in-house foresight capability and realizing successful outcomes. Thus, scanning may represent a dynamic capability for firms (Eisenhardt and Martin, 2000).

The complexity of an external environment in which crisis is widespread and common together with the complexity of an internal environment in which different ways of organizing are emerging at the same time heterogeneity of the workforce is increasing make it critical for firms to have mechanisms in place to scan and interpret their environment. While it is clear that the external environment needs to be scanned, the question is how do organizations do that exactly.

As it was commented in Chapter 3, L'Oréal has a group that is called Development, Trends and Intelligence. One of the responsibilities of this group is to scan the external environment to understand and anticipate trends in the market and in Gen Y's orientation. L'Oréal has thus intensified its interpretation mechanisms to make sure its capacity for responsiveness continues to be fast.

However, formal scanning mechanisms such as that deployed at L'Oréal may not be enough to anticipate changes and provide a fast response. Pettigrew and Whipp (1991) point out that scanning and interpretation happen across the organization. They also argue that it is dangerous to assume that a single specialist alone can come to an accurate interpretation of the entirety of the external environment. Therefore, while formal scanning mechanisms may be useful in scanning the environment, informal scanning mechanisms may also be necessary. For example, firms might have in place not only "monitors" who pay attention to information using trusted information resources but also "viewers" who do not follow a systematic

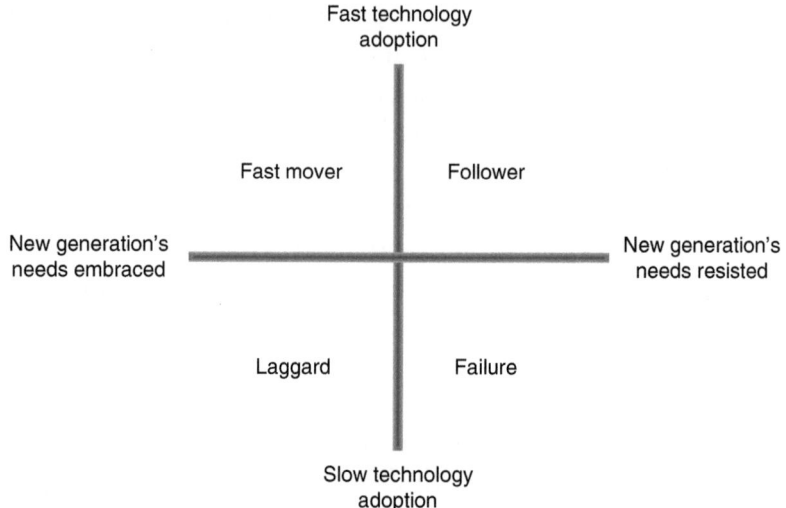

Figure 5.4 *Creating scenarios to anticipate the future (based on Butterfield, 2006)*

approach to scanning (Smith and Raspin, 2011). The idea is that the more people involved in scanning the environment, the more likely firms will anticipate emerging issues and trends in the market.

Butterfield (2006) highlights the value of creating scenarios using two powerful and interesting change drivers to help firms anticipate the future. In particular, he proposes using a matrix that captures the association between the drivers of technology adoption, on the one hand, and the drivers of the response to demographic shifts, on the other. Figure 5.4 presents this matrix.

Each quadrant of the matrix in Figure 5.4 represents different future states of the world that firms need to explore and analyze. The two drivers suggested by Butterfield (2006) help us imagine different ways in which companies can lead the market – from quickly adopting new technologies and embracing the new generation's needs to avoiding both drivers perhaps due to inertial forces within the organization. By creating future scenarios as in the figure, companies can choose the right drivers for their firm and sector.

The capacity to anticipate and respond quickly also requires that people be able to participate in decision-making. Firms need to open their decision-making process to more people in different parts of the decision process, to be infused with new ideas and respond to market needs quickly. Again, the younger generation can bring a fresh outlook to organizations, providing organizations an opportunity to increase their cognitive diversity as well as their scanning effectiveness.

New HR Paradigm

On the subject of the need to change and adapt, Handy (2009: 86) notes that King Charles I was beheaded because he refused to adapt the substance of his role to meet the needs of a changing society. While a detailed discussion of the evolution of HR or HR's involvement in organizational strategy and transformation is outside the scope of this book, it bears mentioning that there is no doubt that HR policies and practices need to be adapted to the real needs of the future organization and its workforce, helping the firm achieve organizational agility and thereby meet its strategic aims and performance objectives.

Katzenbach and Khan (2009) argue that successful organizations of the future will need to work hard to create organizationally dynamic approaches that can integrate the informal organization with the formal organization. HR therefore needs to make sure that it is able to respond to these challenges posed by the future organization and new young workforce.

To achieve organizational agility, a company needs to align its rewards, processes, structure, people practices, values and beliefs (Galbraith, 2009). However, the changes required at both the firm level and the workforce level necessitate a new paradigm to effectively align these factors.

The human and organizational challenges that are described throughout the book underscore the idea of constantly working toward alignment. The practices and processes that HR leaders used as tools to achieve alignment before will not be adequate if we account for the new young workforce having a different mind-set and the future organization being more virtual. In short, traditional HR approaches fall short of the levels of complexity HR will increasingly face.

The new HR paradigm has to replace the traditional practices with new ones. In doing so, the new paradigm should consider not only the organization's strategic objectives but also its culture and purpose, respecting the values and identity of the firm. In particular, the culture and purpose of the organization should infuse the organization's strategy and operations. The HR drivers should thus be built taking into account the previous dimensions, not disconnected from them. That is, the HR drivers should leverage both the firm's culture and its strategy. This implies that the HR dimension of the model in Figure 5.3 can be critical for organizational alignment.

Figure 5.5 summarizes the new paradigm of HR supporting the strategy and organizational culture.

To build a consistent EVP, firms need consistent practices aligned with their values. Few companies are successful in constantly working on their HR drivers to achieve alignment. Natura, the Brazilian beauty firm, was created with this idea in mind. With 2011 revenues of R$5.591 million[3] (US$2.9 billion), Natura is a multinational company that has observed huge growth in Latin America and has created a foothold in Europe (i.e., France). The firm sells beauty products produced using natural resources.

The firm has strong values in which the idea of human well-being (within and outside the organization) is critical. "Well being–being well" is the slogan of the firm and also an important part of its EVP. This slogan captures the company's aim to have a positive impact on both the environment (i.e., the company has made a commitment to neutralize all greenhouse gas emissions, and it launches products based on the sustainable use of Brazil's biodiversity) and its community of employees (i.e., by supporting freedom, participation and sustainability).

Figure 5.6 summarizes Natura's alignment model.

Flávio Pesiguelo, manager of International Organization, Development & Sustainability at Natura, believes that the company's model works because the organization's strong beliefs "are impregnated within the firm and its HR practices are aligned

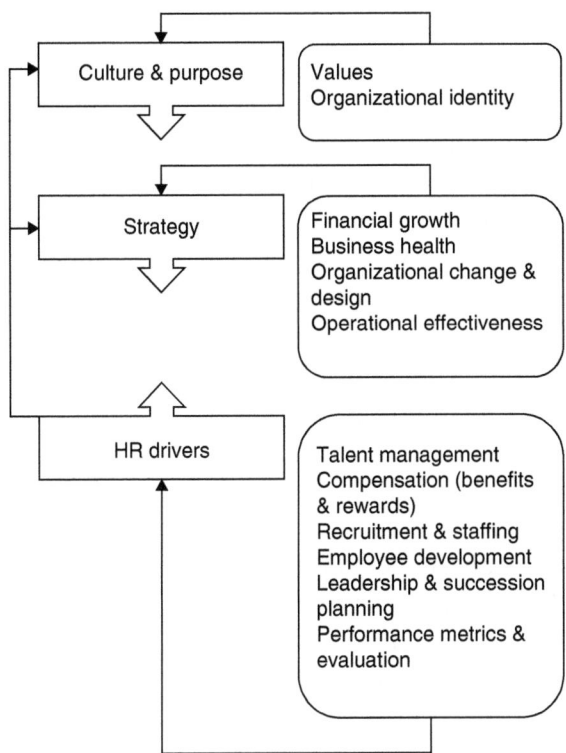

Figure 5.5 *Aligning the organization and the new HR paradigm*

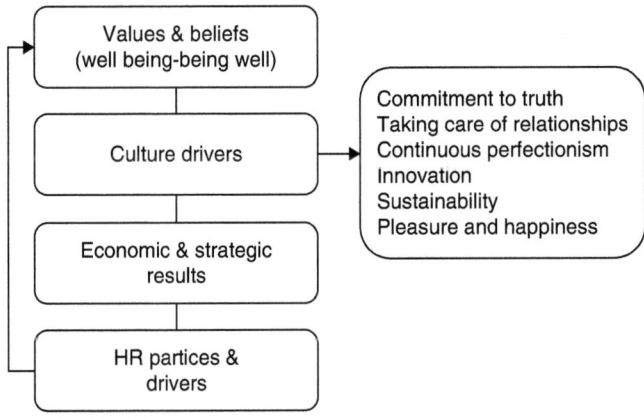

Figure 5.6 *Natura's alignment model*

accordingly."[4] Thus, the new HR paradigm at Natura is infused by the firm's beliefs, and those beliefs lead the firm's culture drivers.

There are various examples of how Natura has changed its HR practices to make sure they are aligned with the company's beliefs and culture drivers. Most firms have a performance/potential matrix. At Natura, the firm has adapted this matrix. As Flávio Pesiguelo explains, "We have the performance/commitment matrix. We found this is coherent. To understand leaders' commitment, we assess four factors: self-knowledge, relationships, sustainability and protagonism."[5]

The most explicit HR practice aligned with the company's beliefs is that related to compensation. Natura employs what it refers to as triple bottom line objectives:

> Our salaries and benefits might be average in the market. But the big difference is that a director or vice president's bonus will be tied to what we call the triple bottom line. This means that managers should meet financial, environmental and social objectives. If in a meeting the environmental benefits are not yet developed, then the financial proposal is not approved.[6]

At Natura, financial objectives focus on EBIDTA (earnings before interest, taxes, depreciation and amortization), environmental objectives focus on the reduction of CO_2 and social objectives focus on the quality of relationships with the workforce (and in particular the sales force) as measured through surveys and interviews.

The new HR paradigm, then, will require that companies align people and organizations to the set of values ingrained in the culture of the firm. This is the most coherent way to achieve alignment, with HR practices and processes conveying those values to employees.

Strong Sense of Purpose

There was a time when organizations were by and large stable. Theories such as the punctuated equilibrium theory characterized sudden, one-time changes that led to deep organizational transformation as revolutions (Romanelli and Tushman, 1994). Once a revolutionary change had been absorbed by a company, a new equilibrium (i.e., stability) emerged, leading to a return to organizational stability and more importantly organizational effectiveness.

Today, however, complexity is the new norm, with organizational change occurring continuously rather than as sudden, one-time events. Rindova and Kotha (2001) refer to the process of continuous transformation as "continuous morphing," a process that facilitates organizations' ability to maintain their competitive advantage when competitive conditions change. So organizations now confront constant change in the market, higher levels of complexity and a deep demographic change that is only starting to take place. The question they face is thus: How can they survive the turmoil ahead; that is, how should firms organize when their external and internal environments both require that they change all the time?

In this book it is argued that a strong sense of purpose is what will anchor firms in the midst of a changing world and in turn help them survive the turmoil. Companies with a strong sense of purpose are "visionary firms," according to Collins and Porras (1991), because they can articulate a core ideology.

But what is behind a firm's core ideology or sense of purpose? – the identity of the organization (Hatum, 2007). Identity, as Lawler III and Worley (2009: 192) explain, "is what keeps organisations from being whip-sawed by environmental demands for change in strategic intent." Organizations that have a strong identity have a clear sense of who they are and what they stand for. Thus, under conditions of external volatility and internal needs to adapt quickly, a strong organizational identity will help anchor people as they face continual change.

AGD, a manufacturer of edible soy oil products based in Argentina with 2011 revenues of US$4 billion, is used to turbulence. One of the worst periods in Argentina's recent economic history was the 1980s, when inflation reached approximately 5,000% in 1989 (INDEC, 1998). Since that time, the company has implemented a number of important changes and today continues a process of constant transformation. For instance, AGD has shifted from a functional structure to a business unit-based structure, from a homogeneous workforce to a diverse workforce and from being a one-product company to a multi-product company. Notwithstanding all of these changes, the firm has remained rooted in its identity and values. As one of the firm's directors explains,

> Over the 1990s the company has changed a lot. However, if you ask an employee whether they have felt the changes, they would say that they had not noticed internal turmoil. They did not feel threatened by the changes. . . . However, if you compare our business now and ten years ago, you would think we were a different company.[7]

As seen in Chapter 1, the future organizations will need to be open to change, adapting their structures to both new technology and new generations of employees who want to see new ways of organizing that cater to their interest in integrating work and life. In addition to changing how they are organized, companies will have to adapt their strategies, products and processes.

How can future firms balance the need for change against the desire for stability? Gustafson and Reger (1995) distinguish two parts of an organization's identity: the intangible attributes that are central and enduring (i.e., the firm's core values), and the substantive attributes that change as in response to changing conditions (i.e., the firm's strategies, products etc.). Thus, in times of rapid change, when organizations need to adapt to the complexity posed by the external and internal environments, the company's sense of purpose – based on its organizational identity and core values – should remain unchanged while its structure, strategy, products and processes should change.

Figure 5.7 summarizes how firms can balance the need for change against the desire for stability.

So firms able to adopt a model in which continuous transformation is combined with stable elements will avoid creating internal turmoil. These companies will be able to offer new ways

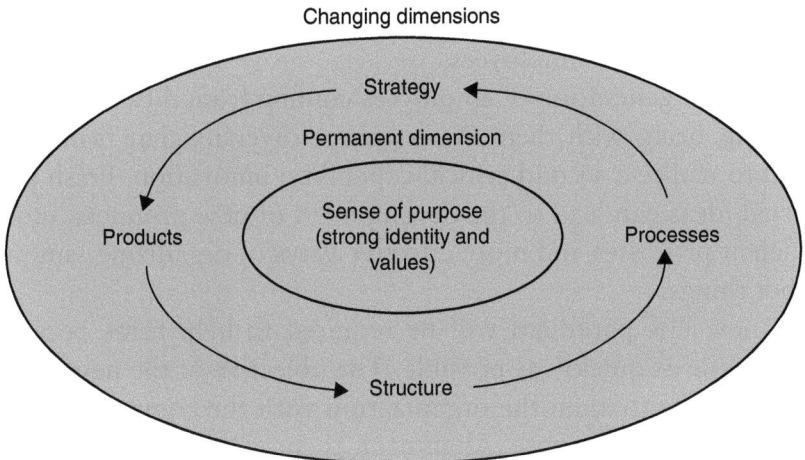

Figure 5.7 *A model of change and stability for the future organization*

of organizing as required by the new workforce, and the new employees will find elements of a long-term proposition supported by strong values.

****

The elements of the model of organizational agility are connected to each other, enhancing firms' ability to adapt quickly under circumstances of rapid change. Organizational agility will provide companies a variety of capabilities that will allow them to survive times of rapid change in both the external environment (e.g., frequent crises and demographic changes) and the internal environment (i.e., more virtuality in day-to-day operations and overlapping generations at work).

Being able to anticipate trends in the external environment will provide the first key capability: the responsiveness necessary to adapt quickly and avoid being a laggard in the market. Most importantly, from the perspective of this book, responsiveness will allow firms to change their way of organizing according to the demands of the market and the needs of the new workforce. By anticipating and responding quickly to generational needs, companies can guarantee their ability to attract and retain the new generation of employees.

The new generation of employees coming from different backgrounds bring with them the cognitive diversity that firms will need to realize a second critical capability: innovation. Fresh and varied ideas can lead to the development of new products, more efficient processes and more effective ways of organizing, among other things.

A new HR paradigm will be required to help firms become more agile as quickly as possible. The objective of the new paradigm will be to align the organization with the company's strategic intent and purpose. Alignment, then, will be a third critical capability needed to support the agility necessary for the future. By using clear and well-adapted practices based on a firm's values, companies may be able to sustain new ways of organizing longer as well as attract and retain new generations of employees, building commitment over the long term.

The sense of purpose mentioned above will provide companies a fourth critical capability: the anchors or coherence their employees will need while working in the midst of constant change. Agile firms need to move fast. To not get lost in the turbulence, then, they need to build a strong identity from which to provide a sense of continuity. Clear values and beliefs will be critical for retaining good talent.

Figure 5.8 summarizes the four capabilities mentioned above in a model of organizing for the future workplace and workforce.

All four dimensions of organizational agility should work in a consistent way, with each dimension consistently supporting the other. High levels of diversity brought by the new generation entering the workforce can enhance a company's ability to innovate and stay ahead of the competition. These innovations may require different HR practices and organizational processes, for example, more flexibility and virtuality. A more virtual firm that increasingly uses social networks might require the expertize of the younger generation, which is more familiar with such technologies. The arrival of this generation may lead to the development of

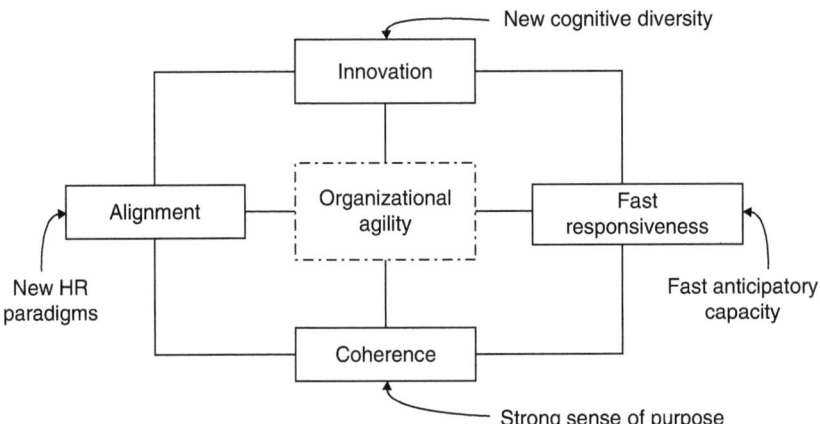

Figure 5.8 *A model of organizing for the future workplace and workforce*

new processes and practices that change how work is conducted throughout the organization, boosting productivity and avoiding organizational inertia.

CONCLUDING REMARKS

In trying to make sense of all the changes organizations will confront in the future, Malone et al. (2003) point to the case of electricity. They note that nearly a half-century was required before the "transforming new technology" would first start to have a significant impact. "Once that impact was felt, however, it turned out to be a sustained one, lasting another half-century" (Malone et al., 2003: 415).

The lag between electricity's discovery and impact can be instructive as we consider the organizational changes discussed in this book – they will not be sudden changes, but gradual ones. However, once these changes have been absorbed by organizations, there will be no going back – they will revolutionize every aspect of every company's organization. Some firms in some industries will try to postpone the various changes described throughout this book to the extent possible, while others are already searching for ways to adapt as quickly as possible. In the end, however, all companies will see changes in how they organize and manage people. It is only a matter of time.

In this book, we have gone back and forth in our discussion of two main subjects: people and organizations. Chapter 1 was focused on new ways of organizing and the importance of organizational agility in an era in which virtuality is relevant. Chapter 5 returned to this topic when it introduced a simple model of organizational agility, a model that also incorporates the analyzes of demographic changes in Chapter 2, new EVPs and new ways of recruiting in Chapter 3, and new learning paradigms, the development of future leaders and the shift in career paths in Chapter 4.

In each chapter, however, the ideas of managing people, on the one hand, and organizing the workplace, on the other, have always been present and interconnected. When talking about new ways of organizing, Chapter 1 also tackled the problems of disaggregated jobs and what is called "virtual people." Chapter 2 related the huge demographic changes ahead to the workplace by analyzing the different generations' characteristics and how each generation separately impacts the organization. Chapter 3 focused on how organizations should build their EVP to attract new talent and motivate existing talent, but in doing so it emphasized that a firm's EVP should take into account characteristics of the future workforce so that the EVP achieves its intended goals over the long term. The same applies to the ideas and practices analyzed with respect to recruiting new employees: While new practices at the organizational level were evaluated, the main rationale was to address the question of how recruitment programs need to adapt to attract the new young workforce. Chapter 4 considered new learning paradigms, the main characteristics of future leaders and new trends in career paths, but each of these discussions also addressed the organizational challenges that the shifts from more traditional processes will represent. In sum, it is very difficult to imagine thinking about how to prepare for organizations' future development without also taking into account generational changes and in turn changes in people management and vice versa.

This period of change in the workplace and workforce calls for an innovative approach to be effective. A continuous transformation process entails new ideas and hence will need to incentivize the creativity that leads to new ideas. A clear agenda for CEOs, managers and HR will also be needed. CEOs' agendas will need to incorporate relevant organizational issues such as the best way to organize the firm to be able to compete into the future against competitors thinking along similar lines. CEOs' agendas will also have to address the changing composition of the workforce, turning the threats into opportunities and adapting to the new workforce's characteristics to leverage their strengths for the benefit of the whole organization.

Managers will need to be able to adapt, becoming transitional leaders able to drive the organizational changes required of the firm and develop the young future leaders. This may be the most difficult challenge of all because failing at this may result in the manager no longer being relevant in the labor market.

Finally, HR will need to view talent supply as a critical concern over the long term. Moreover, HR has to replace old recruiting and retention practices with drivers of change and organizational alignment. The HR area cannot be limited to personnel administration anymore. Rather, it needs to put into place programs that attract, develop and commit the best people for the organization, those who will enhance organizational health, effectiveness and performance, and who will be able to lead the organization in the future.

The future organization will be a thrilling place, although the challenges ahead will be difficult hurdles to jump. There is, however, light at the end of the tunnel: The time is ripe for companies to start exploring those organizational changes and paradigm shifts that will best prepare them to address the generational changes and market turmoil to come, and the rewards for those companies able to anticipate the future of the workplace and the workforce will be significant.

This page intentionally left blank

Interviews

I would like to thank the experts and company managers who had the time and generosity for the interviews and for providing valuable information for this book.

Experts

Ronald Alsop, was editor of *The Wall Street Journal* and *Workforce Management*. He is currently a freelance writer and public speaker focusing on Millennial generation. He is, among others, the author of *The Trophy Kids Grow Up*, Summit, New Jersey, United States

Mary Yoko Brannen, visiting full professor of strategy and management at INSEAD, and founding director of the Institute for Global Learning and Innovation, Fontainebleau, France

Barry Clark, member of the Future Foundation and author of *Vision of Britain 2020*, London, United Kingdom

Rob Salkowitz, consultant specializing in the social implications of new technology and the next-generation workforce. He is the author of *Young World Rising* and *Generation Blend*, Washington, United States

Managers interviewed from the companies and organizations that participated in the research

Ferran Adrià, chef and co-owner of elBulli restaurant, Rosas, Spain

Guillermo Amor, director of training at FC Barcelona, Barcelona, Spain

Marko Balabanovic, head of innovation, Lastminute.com, London, United Kingdom

Tonatiuh Barradas, vice president of Strategic Industries, SAP, Miami, United States

Oriol Castro, kitchen chef and responsible for creativity at elBulli restaurant, Rosas, Spain

Aude Desanges, Talent Recruitment International, L'Oréal, Paris, France

Alex Duncan, head of online development, Lastiminute.com, London, United Kingdom

Carles Folguera, director of La Masía at FC Barcelona, Barcelona, Spain

Jaime Jordana, global corporate director of HR development, Pernod Ricard, Paris, France

Ellen Koning, talent manager for ICT, Rabobkank, Utretch, The Netherlands

Fritz Korten, founder of Frisse Blikken, Utretch, The Netherlands

Géraud-Marie Lacassagne, head of HR, Coty Group, Paris, France

Nick Leopard, founder and co-owner of Accordion Partner, New York, United States

Ginette Martin, regional HR manager of Latin America and Africa, Panamá city, Panamá

Jordi Mestre, member of the board at FC Barcelona and the individual responsible for Initial Football, Barcelona, Spain

Carlos Moncayo, CEO and cofounder of ASIAM Business Group, Hangzhou, China

Julian Nebreda, regional senior vice president, AES, Richmond, United Kingdom

Kay Penney, regional HR manager of Europe and CIS countries, AES, Richmond, United Kingdom

Flávio Pesiguelo, International Organization, Development & Sustainability manager, Natura, Sao Paulo, Brazil

Gabriele Silva, recruitment project manager, L'Oréal, Paris, France

Sebastián Soria, global compensation director, The Dow Chemical Company, Midland, Michigan, United States

Nick Van Dam, global director of Learning, e-Learning Solutions & Technologies, Deloitte Touche Tohmatsu Limited; global client engagement advisor, Human Capital consultant at Deloitte Consulting LLP, Amsterdam, The Netherlands
Francois de Wazières, director of International Recruitment, L'Oréal, Paris, France

The following are people who helped in granting access to the companies:
Constanza Bertorello, Ricardo Falú, Daniel Buzaglo, Santiago Vallé, Alex Abulafia, Marc Cuspinera, Xavier Guarte Serrano, Lola Bou, Ketty Calatayub, Sabine Hoeksema and Facundo Garretón.

This page intentionally left blank

Notes

INTRODUCTION

1. Seeing things as they really are. Interview with Peter Drucker. *Forbes Magazine*. March 10, 1997.

1 ORGANIZING AND THE NEW AGILE AND VIRTUAL FIRM

1. Charles Handy (2009: 90).
2. How Pixar adds a new school of thought to Disney. By W.C. Talylor and P. LeBarre. *The New York Times*. January 26, 2006. http://www.nytimes.com/2006/01/29/business/yourmoney/29pixar.html?pagewanted=all.
3. The emerging case for open business methods. By Dion Hinchcliffe. Enterprise Web 2.0. December 4, 2008. http://www.zdnet.com/blog/hinchcliffe/the-emerging-case-for-open-business-methods/218.
4. http://www.crowdsourcing.com/.
5. http://en.wikipedia.org/wiki/Wikipedia:About.
6. According to Forbes.com, by 2010, Threadless paid winners (more than 300 each year) US$2,000 for their designs.
7. Need to build a community? Learn from Threadless. Social media and loyal fans help this T-shirt company to thrive. By Laurie Burkitt. Forbes.com. January 7, 2010. http://www.forbes.com/2010/01/06/threadless-t-shirt-community-crowdsourcing-cmo-network-threadless.html.
8. Creating a brand for a new business. By Kris Ruby. *The Wall Street Journal*/Small Business. US edition. October 14, 2010.

http://online.wsj.com/article/SB10001424052748703727804576017432429971442.html#articleTabs%3Darticle.
9. In search of innovation. By J. Bessant, K. Möleim and B. Von Stamm. *The Wall Street Journal*. Page R4 (Business). June 22, 2009. http://online.wsj.com/article/SB20001424052970204830304574133562888635626.html?KEYWORDS=innocentive.
10. http://www.innocentive.com.
11. InnoCentive.com Case Study, Harvard Business School. By K.R. Lakhani. October 28, 2009.
12. Cited by D. Kirkpatrick (2010: 287).
13. Charles Handy (2009: 89).
14. By Barry Clark, member of the Future Foundation (http://www.futurefoundation.net) and author of *Vision of Britain 2020* published by the Future Foundation, 2010, London, United Kingdom.
15. Interview with Ferran Adrià, chef and co-owner of elBulli restaurant, Rosas, Spain.
16. ElBulli, a far-out-place. Case study written by Professor Andrés Hatum (2010). Published by IAE Business School, Universidad Austral, Pilar, Buenos Aires, Argentina.
17. Interview with Ferran Adrià, chef and co-owner of elBulli restaurant, Rosas, Spain.
18. Interview with Ferran Adrià, chef and co-owner of elBulli restaurant, Rosas, Spain.
19. Interview with Oriol Castro, chef responsible for creativity at elBulli restaurant, Rosas, Spain.
20. Interview with Ferran Adrià, chef and co-owner of elBulli restaurant. Interview held in Buenos Aires, Argentina.
21. Interview with Ferran Adrià, chef and co-owner of elBulli restaurant. Interview held in Buenos Aires, Argentina.

2 DEMOGRAPHIC CHANGES IN THE WORKPLACE

1. How BMW deals with an aging workforce. By Richard Roth. CBSNews. September 5, 2010. http://www.cbsnews.com/stories/2010/09/05/sunday/main6837469.shtml.

2. How BMW deals with an aging workforce. By Richard Roth. CBSNews. September 5, 2010. http://www.cbsnews.com/stories/2010/09/05/sunday/main6837469.shtml.
3. The silver tsunami: Business will have to learn how to manage an ageing workforce. *The Economist*, Shumpeter section. February 4, 2010. http://www.economist.com/node/15450864.
4. How young people view their lives, future and politics. A portrait of "Generation Next". The Pew Research Center for the People and the Press (2007). Washington DC. http://www.peoople-press.org.
5. Does your company have an IT generation gap? By G.A. Curtis, K. Dempski and C.S. Farley (2009). Published in *Outlook*, the journal of high-performance business of Accenture. Number 1. http://www.accenture.com/us-en/outlook/pages/outlook-journal-2009-workplace-technology.aspx.
6. http://www.cirquedusoleil.com/en/about/global-citizenship/workplace/conditions.aspx.
7. http://www.cirquedusoleil.com/en/about/global-citizenship/default.aspx.
8. http://www.cirquedusoleil.com/en/about/global-citizenship/community/social-circus/cirque-du-monde.aspx.
9. Social networking comes to age. By Joe Leahy. F.T.com (Technology section). September 1, 2010. http://www.ft.com/cms/s/0/f2080bec-b5f3-11df-a048-00144feabdc0.html#axzz1k0LhXsUd.
10. From conflict to "cohorts": When young and older workers mix. By Emilie Le Beau. *Workforce Management*. October 2010, p. 12.
11. Talking about whose generation? By D. Hole, L. Zhong and J. Schwarts (2010). *Deloitte Review*. Issue 6, pp. 83–97.
12. www.asiam.com.cn.
13. Interview with Carlos Moncayo, CEO and cofounder of ASIAM Business Group, Hangzhou, China.
14. Interview with Carlos Moncayo, CEO and cofounder of ASIAM Business Group, Hangzhou, China.
15. Interview with Carlos Moncayo, CEO and cofounder of ASIAM Business Group, Hangzhou, China.

16. http://www.deloitte.com/view/en_GX/global/about/index.htm (accessed August 27, 2012).
17. Interview with Nick Van Dam, global director Learning, e-Learning Solutions & Technologies, Deloitte Touche Tohmatsu Limited, Amsterdam, The Netherlands.
18. Interview with Nick Van Dam, Global Director Learning, e-Learning Solutions & Technologies, Deloitte Touche Tohmatsu Limited, Amsterdam, The Netherlands.
19. Interview with Nick Van Dam, Global Director Learning, e-Learning Solutions & Technologies, Deloitte Touche Tohmatsu Limited, Amsterdam, The Netherlands.
20. Global Workforce Study reports: How far, how fast and how enduring. Towers Watson (2010). New York. http://www.google.com.ar/url?sa=t&rct=j&q=&esrc=s&frm=1&source=web&cd=2&ved=0CEYQFjAB&url=http%3A%2F%2Fwww.unav.es%2Ficf%2Fmain%2Ftop%2F2010%2FTowers_Global-Workfoce-Study-2010.pdf&ei=pznHUMa8MoKg9QSjqYDoCg&usg=AFQjCNHRBw0zloccH56BUZBKTOJZx9yNdg&sig2=oU75yzb1nqBcKPts2kAZMA.
21. Jumping the boundaries of corporate IT. Accenture global research on Millennials' use of technology (2010). http://nstore.accenture.com/technology/millennials/global_millennial_generation_research.pdf.
22. Interview with Mary Yoko Brannen, visiting full professor of strategy and management at INSEAD, Fontainebleau, France. Professor Brannen is a founding director of the Institute for Global Learning and Innovation.
23. www.fresh-forces.com.
24. Interview with Fritz Korten, CEO, Frisse Blikken, Utretch, The Netherlands.
25. Interview with Fritz Korten, CEO, Frisse Blikken, Utretch, The Netherlands.
26. Interview with Fritz Korten, CEO, Frisse Blikken, Utretch, The Netherlands.
27. Interview with Fritz Korten, CEO, Frisse Blikken, Utretch, The Netherlands.
28. Interview with Fritz Korten, CEO, Frisse Blikken, Utretch, The Netherlands.

3 ATTRACTING MILLENNIALS TO THE WORKPLACE

1. Interview with Francois de Wazières, director of International Recruitment, L'Oréal, Paris.
2. The employee value proposition: How to be an employer of choice. By S. Black (2009). http://knowledge.insead.edu/contents/Black.cfm (accessed March 22, 2011).
3. Why an employee value proposition matters: Creating alignment, engagement and stronger business results. By K. Kibbe, L. Sejen and K. Yates. Tower Watson (October 13, 2010). http://www.shrm.org/multimedia/webcasts/Documents/11evp.pdf.
4. http://www.universumglobal.com/IDEAL-Employer-Rankings/Global-Top-50.aspx.
5. http://www.universumglobal.com/IDEAL-Employer-Rankings/The-National-Editions/American-Student-Survey (accessed June 7, 2012).
6. http://www.universumglobal.com/IDEAL-Employer-Rankings/The-National-Editions/French-Student-Survey (accessed June 7, 2012).
7. http://www.universumglobal.com/IDEAL-Employer-Rankings/The-National-Editions/UK-Student-Survey (accessed June 7, 2012).
8. Millennials at work. Reshaping the workplace. PricewaterhouseCoopers (2011). http://www.pwc.com/gx/en/managing-tomorrows-people/future-of-work/download.jhtml (accessed August 10, 2012).
9. How multinationals can attract the talent they need. By M. Dewhurst, M. Pettigrew and R. Srinivasan (2012). *McKinsey Quarterly*. Issue, June.
10. http://money.cnn.com/magazines/fortune/mostadmired/2011/full_list/.
11. Managing tomorrow's people. Millennials at work: Perspectives from a new generation. PricewaterhouseCoopers (2008). http://www.pwc.com/gx/en/managing-tomorrows-people/future-of-work/pdf/mtp-millennials-at-work.pdf (accessed August 10, 2012). Check also http://www.pwc.com/managingpeople2020 for further information and reports on Millennials.

12. http://www.aes.com/aes/index?page=home.
13. Interview with Kay Penney, regional HR manager for Europe and CIS countries, AES, Richmond, United Kingdom.
14. Interview with Julian Nebreda, senior regional vice president, AES, Richmond, United Kingdom.
15. Interview with Kay Penney, regional HR manager for Europe and CIS countries, AES, Richmond, United Kingdom.
16. Interview with regional HR manager, AES, Panamá City, Panamá.
17. http://www.teachforamerica.org.
18. http://www.teachforamerica.org/our-organization.
19. A chosen few are Teaching for America. By Michael Winerip. *The New York Times* (Education section). July 10, 2010. http://www.nytimes.com/2010/07/12/education/12winerip.html.
20. CRM (Customer Relationship Management) is a type of software, often used in sales environments.
21. http://www.salesforce.com/company/foundation/.
22. What Gen Y really wants. By Penelope Trunk. *The Times* (Global Business section). July 5, 2007. http://www.time.com/time/magazine/article/0,9171,1640395,00.html (accessed March 22, 2011).
23. Talent Mobility 2020. The next generation of international assignments. PricewaterhouseCoopers (2010). http://www.pwc.com/gx/en/managing-tomorrows-people/future-of-work/download.jhtml (accessed August 10, 2012).
24. Interview with Francois de Wazières, director of International Recruitment, L'Oréal, Paris.
25. http://www.peacecorps.gov/.
26. http://www.sap.com/index.epx# (accessed August 6, 2012).
27. Interview with Tonatiuh Barradas, vice president of Strategic Industries for Latin America, SAP, Miami, United States.
28. Interview with Tonatiuh Barradas, vice president of Strategic Industries for Latin America, SAP, Miami, United States.
29. Millennials at work. Reshaping the workplace. PricewaterhouseCoopers (2011). http://www.pwc.com/gx/en/managing-tomorrows-people/future-of-work/download.jhtml (accessed August 10, 2012).

30. Interview with Nick Van Dam, global director for learning for Deloitte Touche Tohmatsu and director of human capital for Deloitte Consulting, Amsterdam, The Netherlands.
31. How multinationals can attract the talent they need. By M. Dewhurst, M. Pettigrew and R. Srinivasan (2012). *McKinsey Quarterly*. Issue, June.
32. http://www.tata.com/aboutus/sub_index.aspx?sectid=8hOk5Qq3EfQ= (accessed August 6, 2012).
33. How multinationals can attract the talent they need. By M. Dewhurst, M. Pettigrew and R. Srinivasan (2012). *McKinsey Quarterly*. Issue, June.
34. Reinvent opportunity: Looking through a new lens. IWD Survey. November 2010. Accenture. http://www.accenture.com/SiteCollectionDocuments/PDF/Accenture_IWD_Research_Embargoed_until_March_4_2011.pdf.
35. Despite low job satisfaction, employees unlikely to seek new jobs. Accenture Research Reports. March 4, 2011. http://newsroom.accenture.com/article_display.cfm?article_id=5163.
36. Interview with Kay Penney, regional HR manager for Europe and CIS countries, AES, Richmond, United Kingdom.
37. What Gen Y really wants. By Penelope Trunk. *The Times* (Global Business section). July 5, 2007. http://www.time.com/time/magazine/article/0,9171,1640395,00.html (accessed March 22, 2011).
38. http://www.coty.com/#/about_coty/facts.
39. Interview with Géraud-Marie Lacassagne, head of HR Coty Group, Paris, France.
40. Interview with Géraud-Marie Lacassagne, head of HR Coty Group, Paris, France.
41. Interview with Géraud-Marie Lacassagne, head of HR Coty Group, Paris, France.
42. Interview with Géraud-Marie Lacassagne, head of HR Coty Group, Paris, France.
43. Interview with Géraud-Marie Lacassagne, head of HR Coty Group, Paris, France.
44. Interview with Géraud-Marie Lacassagne, head of HR Coty Group, Paris, France.

45. Employee engagement. A leading indicator of financial performance. *Gallup Management Journal.* June 8, 2011. http://www.gallup.com/consulting/52/employee-engagement.aspx.
46. A threat to German growth. By Marco Nink and Bryant Ott. Gallup (2011). http://gmj.gallup.com/content/147875/Threat-German-Growth.aspx.
47. Employee engagement report 2011. Beyond the numbers: A practical approach for individuals, managers and executives. Blessing White Research. New Jersey, United States. http://www.blessingwhite.com/EEE__report.asp.
48. Survey report: Innovation in the workplace. How are organizations responding to Generation Y employees and Web 2.0 technologies? Chartered Institute of Personnel and Development (September 2008), London, United Kingdom. http://www.peixunjie.com/upload_files/article/201206/191.pdf.
49. http://www.pg.com/en_US/careers/hiring_process.shtml.
50. Dream jobs: College students get real. *Bloomberg Business Week.* By Francesca Di Meglio. April 30, 2010. http://www.businessweek.com/managing/content/apr2010/ca20100428_482088_page_2.htm (accessed March 9, 2011).
51. http://www.experiencepg.com/default.aspx.
52. http://www.experiencepg.com/social-networks.aspx.
53. Interview with Gabriele Silva, recruitment project manager. Development, Trends and Intelligence Department at L'Oréal, Paris.
54. Interview with Gabriele Silva, recruitment project manager. Development, Trends and Intelligence Department at L'Oréal, Paris.
55. Interview with Gabriele Silva, recruitment project manager. Development, Trends and Intelligence Department at L'Oréal, Paris.
56. Interview with Gabriele Silva, recruitment project manager. Development, Trends and Intelligence Department at L'Oréal, Paris.
57. http://www.sodexo.com/group_en/default2.asp.
58. http://careers.sodexousa.com/content/sodexocareers/.

59. http://careers.sodexousa.com/?utm_source=careersite&utm_campaign=opportunities.
60. How multinationals can attract the talent they need. By M. Dewhurst, M. Pettigrew and R. Srinivasan (2012). *McKinsey Quarterly*. Issue, June.
61. http://www.amctheatres.com/ (accessed April 8, 2011).
62. http://www.amctheatres.com/careers/?WT.mc_id=nh_about (accessed April 8, 2011).
63. http://about.zappos.com/ (accessed April 8, 2011).
64. http://twitter.com/inside_zappos (accessed April 8, 2011).
65. Got talent? Competing to hire the best and motivate the rest. Special report: The future of jobs. *The Economist*. September 10, 2010.
66. www.clifbar.com/soul/who_we_are (accessed February 11, 2012).
67. Mind the gap: The changing motivations of the UK workforce. Hyphen Recruitment Outsourcing (2010), London, United Kingdom. http://www.hyphen.com/SiteCollectionDocuments/Mind-the-gap-a-hyphen-white-paper.pdf.
68. http://www.dow.com/about/ (accessed May 29, 2012).
69. Interview with Sebastián Soria, global compensation director, The Dow Chemical Company, Midland, Michigan, United States.
70. Cisco connected world technology report 2011. Published by Cisco. http://www.cisco.com/en/US/solutions/ns341/ns525/ns537/ns705/ns1120/2011-CCWTR-Chapter-3-All-Finding.pdf (accessed January 21, 2012).
71. http://www.mcdonalds.com/us/en/careers/working_here/interview_tips.html.
72. Interview with Francois de Wazières, director of International Recruitment, L'Oréal, Paris.
73. Information provided by the company. L'Oréal FIT in a nutshell. Follow-up and Integration Track. Two years of personal guidance and training. Published by Human Resources Group, L'Oréal.
74. http://www.sustainabledevelopment.loreal.com/talent/managing-our-people.asp.

75. Interview with Ronald Alsop. He was editor of *The Wall Street Journal* and of *Workforce Management* (http://www.workforce.com/). He has written many books, including *The Trophy Kids Grow Up* (2008) (http://www.thetrophykids.com).
76. http://www.loreal.com/_en/_ww/html/our-company/facts-figures.aspx? (accessed May 30, 2012).
77. http://www.reveal-thegame.com/default.aspx (accessed January 23, 2012).
78. Interview with Aude Desanges, Talent Recruitment International, L'Oréal, Paris.
79. Interview with Aude Desanges, Talent Recruitment International, L'Oréal, Paris.
80. Interview with Francois de Wazières, director of International Recruitment, L'Oréal, Paris.
81. Interview with Aude Desanges, Talent Recruitment International, L'Oréal, Paris.
82. Interview with Gabriele Silva, recruitment project manager, L'Oréal, Paris.
83. Interview with Francois de Wazières, director of International Recruitment, L'Oréal, Paris.

4   NEW LEARNING PARADIGMS AND THE CHALLENGE OF DEVELOPING THE FUTURE LEADERS

1. http://www.bus.wisc.edu/alc/ (accessed January 23, 2012).
2. http://careers.deloitte.com/united-states/experienced-professionals/culture_education.aspx?CountryContentID=16045 (accessed January 23, 2012).
3. http://www.bp.com/sectiongenericarticle.do?categoryId=3&contentId=2006926 (accessed January 23, 2012).
4. http://www.lastminute.com/site/help/about_us/about-us.html (accessed January 23, 2012).
5. Interview with Marko Balabanovic, head of innovation, Lastminute.com, London, United Kingdom.
6. Interview with Alex Duncan, head of online development, Lastminute.com, London, United Kingdom.
7. Interview with Marko Balabanovic, head of innovation, Lastminute.com, London, United Kingdom.

8. Interview with Marko Balabanovic, head of innovation, Lastminute.com, London, United Kingdom.
9. http://developer.yahoo.com/hackday/ (accessed January 23, 2012).
10. Interview with Marko Balabanovic, head of innovation, Lastminute.com, London, United Kingdom.
11. Interview with Marko Balabanovic, head of innovation, Lastminute.com, London, United Kingdom.
12. Employee engagement report 2011. Beyond the numbers: A practical approach for individuals, managers and executives. Blessing White Research. New Jersey, United States. http://www.blessingwhite.com/EEE__report.asp (accessed January 24, 2012).
13. http://www.rabobank.com/content/about_us/ (accessed January 24, 2012).
14. Interview with Ellen Koning, talent manager for ICT, Rabobank, Utretch, The Netherlands.
15. Interview with Ellen Koning, talent manager for ICT, Rabobank, Utretch, The Netherlands.
16. Interview with Ellen Koning, talent manager for ICT, Rabobank, Utretch, The Netherlands.
17. Interview with Ellen Koning, talent manager for ICT, Rabobank, Utretch, The Netherlands.
18. Developing Chinese leaders in the 21st century. Research overview. Center for Creative Leadership. September 2009, Greensboro, NC. http://www.ccl.org/leadership/pdf/research/DevelopingChineseLeaders.pdf.
19. Developing future leaders for high-growth Indian companies: New perspectives. Center for Creative Leadership. July 2008. Greensboro, NC. http://www.ccl.org/leadership/pdf/research/DevelopingFutureLeaders.pdf.
20. Annual Report 2010/2011. Pernod Ricard. http://www.pernod-ricard.com/ (accessed May 30, 2012).
21. Interview with Jaime Jordana, global corporate director of HR development, Pernod Ricard, Paris, France.
22. Interview with Jaime Jordana, global corporate director of HR development, Pernod Ricard, Paris, France.
23. Interview with Jaime Jordana, global corporate director of HR development, Pernod Ricard, Paris, France.

24. Interview with Jaime Jordana, global corporate director of HR development, Pernod Ricard, Paris, France.
25. Interview with Rob Salkowitz, author of *Young World Rising* and *Generation Blend* and consultant specializing in the social implications of new technology and the next-generation workforce.
26. Motivating Gen Ys in a downturn. By Penelope Trunk. *Bloomberg Businessweek*. June 9, 2009. http://www.businessweek.com/managing/content/jun2009/ca2009069_851860.htm (accessed May 30, 2012).
27. Finesse a flexible work schedule. By Dana Hudepohl. *The Wall Street Journal* (Career section). February 19, 2008. http://online.wsj.com/article/SB120069280250501277.html (accessed January 24, 2012).
28. www.jetblue.com (accessed January 24, 2012).
29. www.accordionpartners.com (accessed January 24, 2012).
30. New model for work–life balance in Wall Street? By Kyle Stock. Wall Street Journal Blogs. January 3, 2011. http://blogs.wsj.com/juggle/2011/01/03/the-jungle-new-model-for-work-life-balance-on-wall-street/?KEYWORDS=work+life+balance (accessed January 24, 2012).
31. Interview with Nick Leopard, founder and co-owner of Accordion Partners, New York, United States.
32. Interview with Nick Leopard, founder and co-owner of Accordion Partners, New York, United States.
33. Interview with Nick Leopard, founder and co-owner of Accordion Partners, New York, United States.
34. Interview with Nick Leopard, founder and co-owner of Accordion Partners, New York, United States.
35. Interview with Nick Leopard, founder and co-owner of Accordion Partners, New York, United States.
36. Career paths: Mapping, ladders and lattices. By Caela Farren, PhD. MasteryWorks, Inc. November 2008. http://www.masteryworks.com/newsite/clientimpact/impact_archives_nov08.html (accessed January 24, 2012).
37. Lionel Messi's final goal. By Bobby Ghosh. *Times Magazine*. February 6, 2012. Pages 22–25.

38. www.fcbarcelona.com/club/history (accessed February 14, 2012).
39. Interview with Jordi Mestre, board member at FC Barcelona and the individual responsible for Initial Football, Barcelona, Spain.
40. Interview with Carles Folguera, director of La Masía at FC Barcelona, Barcelona, Spain.
41. Interview with Guillermo Amor, director of football training at FC Barcelona, Barcelona, Spain.
42. Interview with Carles Folguera, director of La Masía at FC Barcelona, Barcelona, Spain.
43. Interview with Carles Folguera, director of La Masía at FC Barcelona, Barcelona, Spain.
44. Interview with Guillermo Amor, director of football training at FC Barcelona, Barcelona, Spain.

5 THE NEW REALIGNMENT CONTRACT

1. Millennials are rocking the workplace. By L. Lancaster, D. Fiterman and D. Stillman. *TCB Magazine*. June 2010. www.tcbmag.com/industriestrends/humanresources/128806p1.aspx (accessed February 12, 2012).
2. Generation Y goes to work. *The Economist*. December 30, 2008. www.economist.com/node/12863573 (accessed February 12, 2012).
3. http://natura.infoinvest.com.br/enu/4036/RA2011_CompletoGRI_ingles_final.pdf (accessed May 30, 2012).
4. Interview with Flávio Pesiguelo, manager of International Organization, Development & Sustainability, Natura, Brazil.
5. Interview with Flávio Pesiguelo, manager of International Organization, Development & Sustainability, Natura, Brazil.
6. Interview with Flávio Pesiguelo, manager of International Organization, Development & Sustainability, Natura, Brazil.
7. Interview with the director of AGD (in Hatum, 2007: 179).

This page intentionally left blank

Bibliography

Alsop, R. (2008). *The trophy kids grow up. How the Millennial generation is shaking up the workplace.* San Francisco, CA: Jossey Bass.
Anderson, P., & Tushman, M.L. (1990). Technological discontinuities and dominant designs: A cyclical model of technological change. *Administrative Science Quarterly*, 35: 604–633.
Argyris, C., & Schön, D.A. (1999). *On organizational learning.* Second edition. Oxford, UK: Blackwell.
Arthur, M.B., & Rousseau, D.M. (1996). Introduction. In *The boundaryless career. A new employment principle for a new organizational era.* Chapter 1. (eds Arthur, M.B. & Rousseau, D.M.). Oxford: Oxford University Press.
Baker, J. (1998). Find stability in a changing market. *Computer Reseller News*, 777: 61–62.
Barney, J. (1991). Firm resources and sustained competitive advantage. *Journal of Management*, 17 (1): 99–120.
Becker, B.E., Huselid, M.A. & Spratt, M.F. (1997). HR as a source of shareholder value: Research and recommendations. *Human Resource Management*, 36 (1): 39–47.
Benko, C., & Anderson, M. (2010). *The corporate lattice. Achieving high performance in the changing world of work.* Boston, MA: Harvard Business Review Press.
Benko, C., & Weisberg, A. (2007). *Mass Career Customization. Aligning the workplace with today's nontraditional workforce.* Boston, MA: Harvard Business School Press.
Bingham, T., & Conner, M. (2010). *The new social learning. A guide to transforming organizations through social media.* San Francisco, CA: Berrett-Koehler.

Black, S. (2007). The employee value proposition: How to be an employer of choice. Insead Knowledge http://knowledge.insead.edu/leadership-management/talent-management/the-employee-value-proposition-2127 (Accessed 29/11/2012).

Blau, J.R., & McKinley, W. (1979). Ideas, complexity, and innovation. *Administrative Science Quarterly*, 24 (2): 200–219.

Brown, S.L., & Eisenhardt, K.M. (1997). The art of continuous change: Linking complexity theory and time-paced evolution in relentlessly shifting organizations. *Administrative Science Quarterly*, 42: 1–34.

Butterfield, B. (2006). Defining the future. The Forbes Group. www.forbergroup.com/upoads/article/define_the_future-pdf.

Campbell, A. (1998). The agile enterprise: Assessing the technology management issues. *International Journal of Technology Management*, 15 (½): 82–95.

Chandler, A.D. Jr. (1962). *Strategy and structure. Chapters in the history of the American industrial enterprise.* Cambridge, MA: MIT Press.

Chandler, A.D. Jr with the assistance of Takashi Hikino (1990). *Scale and scope: The dynamics of industrial capitalism.* Cambridge, MA: Belknap Press of the Harvard University Press.

Chesbrough, H. (2006). *Open business models.* Boston, MA: Harvard Business School Press.

Christian, P.H., Govande, W., Staehle, W. & Zimmers, E.W. Jr (1999). Advantage through agility. *IIE Solutions*, 31 (11): 28–33.

Collins, J.C., & Porras, J.I. (1991). Organizational vision and visionary organizations. *California Management Review*, 34 (1): 30–52.

Daft, R., & Weick, K.E. (1984). Toward a model of organizations as interpretation systems. *Academy of Management Review*, 9 (2): 284–295.

D'Angelo, M.K. (2009). Gen M: Whose kids are they anyway? In *Teaching Generation M. A handbook for librarians and educators* (eds Bowman Cvetkovic, V. & Lackie, R.J.). Chapter 5, pp. 97–108. New York: Neal-Schuman.

D'Aveni, R.A. (1994). *Hyper-competition.* New York: The Free Press.
Dewhurst, M., Pettigrew, M., & Srinivasan, R. (2012). How multinationals can attract the talent they need. The McKinsey Quarterly. Issue, June.
Dove, R. (1995). Agile benefits: Viability and leadership. *Production,* 107 (4): 20.
Drucker, P.F. (1999). *Innovation and entrepreneurship: Practice and principles.* Oxford, UK: Butterworth and Heinemann.
Dychtwald, K., Erickson, T.J. & Morison, R. (2006). *Workforce crisis. How to beat the coming shortage of skills and talent.* Boston, MA: Harvard Business School Press.
Dyer, L., & Shafer, R. (2003). Dynamic organizations: Achieving marketplace. In *Leading and managing people in the dynamic organization* (eds Peterson, R.S. & Mannix, E.A.). Chapter 2. pp. 7–41. Mahwah, NJ: Lawrence Erlbaum.
Eisenhardt, K.M., & Martin, J.A. (2000). Dynamic capabilities: What are they? *Strategic Management Journal,* 21 (Special Issue): 1105–1121.
Eisenhardt, K.M., & Tabrizi, B.N. (1995). Accelerating adaptive processes: Product innovation in the global computer industry. *Administrative Science Quarterly,* 40: 84–110.
Elmore, T. (2010). *Generation iY. Our last chance to save their future.* Atlanta, GA: Poet Gardener.
Espinoza, C., Ukleja, M., & Rusch, C. (2010). *Managing the Millennials. Discover the core competencies for managing today's workforce.* Hoboken, NJ: John Wiley.
Evans, S.J. (1991). Strategic flexibility for high technology manoeuvres: A conceptual framework. *Journal of Management Studies,* 28 (1): 69–89.
Farber, H.S. (2008). Employment insecurity: The decline in worker–firm attachment in the United States. Working Paper #530. July. Princeton, NJ: Princeton University. Industrial Relations section.
Farrow, D. (2012). Identifying and developing skill expertise. Understanding current limits and exploring future possibilities. In *Talent identification and development in sport.*

International perspectives (eds Baker, J., Cobley, S. & Schorer, J.). Chapter 5. Abingdon, Oxon: Routledge.

Ferriss, T. (2009). *The 4-hour workweek: Escape 9–5, live anywhere, and join the new rich.* New York: Crown Publishing.

Floyd, S.W., & Lane, P.J. (2000). Strategizing throughout the organization: Managing role conflict in strategic renewal. *Academy of Management Review*, 25 (1): 154–177.

Fulmer, R.M., & Bleak, J.L. (2008). *The leadership advantage: How the best companies are developing their talent to pave the way for future success.* New York: Amacom.

Galbraith, J.R. (2009). Multidimensional, multinational organizations of the future. In *The organization of the future 2: Visions, strategies, and insights on managing in a new era* (eds Hessenlbein, F. & Goldsmith, M.). Part 3, Chapter 15. San Francisco, CA: Jossey Bass.

Gergen, C., & Vanourek, G. (2009). Dynamic organizations for an entrepreneurial age. In *The organization of the future 2: Visions, strategies, and insights on managing in a new era* (eds Hessenlbein, F. & Goldsmith, M.). Chapter 9. San Francisco, CA: Jossey Bass.

Gladwell, M. (2008). *Outliers. The story of success.* New York: Little, Brown and Company.

Global Workforce Study: How far, how fast and how enduring. Towers Watson (2010). New York, USA.

Goldman, S.L., Nagel, R.N. & Preiss, K. (1995). *Agile competitors and virtual organizations.* New York: Van Nostrand Reinhold.

Goldsmith, M. (2008). The long view. *Training + Development*, 62 (5). Accessed at http://news-business.vlex.com/source/training-development-3900/issue_nbr/%2362%235.

Goranson, H.T. (1999). *The agile virtual enterprise.* Westport, CT: Quorum Books.

Gossieaux, F., & Moran, E.K. (2010). *The hyper-social organization. Eclipse your competition by leveraging social media.* eBook. New York: McGraw-Hill.

Grantham, C. (2000). *The future of work.* eBook. New York: McGraw-Hill.

Grantham, C., Ware, J.P. & Williamson, C. (2007). *Corporate agility: A new model for competing in a flat world.* New York: Amacom.

Gratton, L. (2011). *The shift. The future of work is already here.* London: Harper Collins.

Gustafson, L.T., & Reger, R.K. (1995). Using organizational identity to achieve stability and change in high velocity environments. Academy of Management Best Papers Proceedings, pp. 464–468.

Guthridge, M., Asmus B.K., & Lawson, E. (2008). Making talent a strategic priority. McKinsey Quarterly. Issue 8. http://www.mckinseyquarterly.com/Making_talent_a_strategic_priority_2092 (Accessed 28/11/2012)

Haeckel, S.H. (1999). *Adaptive enterprise.* Boston, MA: Harvard Business School Press.

Hamel, G. (2007). The Future of Management. Boston: Harvard Business School Press.

Hamel, G., & Breen, B. (2007). *The future of management.* Boston, MA: Harvard Business School Press.

Handy, C. (1989). *The age of unreason.* London: Random House.

Handy, C. (1994). *The empty raincoat: Making sense of the future.* London: Hutchinson.

Handy, C. (2009). Revisiting the concept of the corporation. In *The organization of the future 2: Visions, strategies, and insights on managing in a new era* (eds Hessenlbein, F. & Goldsmith, M.). Chapter 8. pp. 86–97. San Francisco, CA: Jossey-Bass.

Hatum, A. (2007). *Adaptation or expiration in family firms. Determinants of organizational flexibility in emerging economies.* Cheltenham, UK: Edward Elgar.

Hatum, A. (2010). *Next generational talent management. Talent management to survive turmoil.* Hampshire, UK: Palgrave Macmillan.

Hedlund, G. (1994). A model of knowledge management and the N-form corporation. *Strategic Management Journal,* 15: 73–90.

Howe, J. (2008). *Crowdsourcing.* New York: Three Rivers Press.
Howe, N. & Strauss, W. (2000). *Millennials Rising.* The next great generation. New York: Vingage Books
Hugos, M.H. (2009). *Business agility: Sustainable prosperity in a relentlessly competitive world.* Hoboken, NJ: John Wiley.
Illeris, K. (2011). *The fundamentals of workplace learning. Understanding how people learn in working life.* ebook. Abingdon, Oxon: Routledge.
INDEC (Instituto Nacional de Estadisticas y Censos). (1998). *Statistical yearbook of the Argentine Republic 1998.* Buenos Aires: INDEC.
Jamrog, J. (2002). The coming decade of the employee. *Human Resource Planning,* 25 (3): 5.
Johnson, B.C., Mayika, J.M. & Yee, L. (2005). The next revolution in interactions. *McKinsey Quarterly,* 4: 20–33.
Katzenbach, J.R., & Khan, Z. (2009). Mobilizing emotions for performance. In *The organization of the future 2: Visions, strategies, and insights on managing in a new era* (eds Hessenlbein, F. & Goldsmith, M.). Chapter 9. San Francisco, CA: Jossey-Bass.
Keller, S., & Price, C. (2011). *Beyond performance. How great organizations build ultimate competitive advantage.* Hoboken, NJ: John Wiley.
Kirkpatrick, D. (2010). *The Facebook effect. The inside story of the company that is connecting the world.* New York: Simon & Schuster.
Kivenko, K. (1995). Leading your organization to reduced cycle time and increased agility. *The CMA Magazine,* 69 (5): 4.
Knapp, J. (2009). Google and Wikipedia: Friends or foes? In *Teaching Generation M. A handbook for librarians and educators* (eds Bowman Cvetkovic, V. & Lackie, R.J.). Chapter 5, pp. 97–108. New York: Neal-Schuman.
Lancaster, L.C., & Stillman, D. (2010). *The M-factor. How the Millennial generation is rocking the workplace.* New York: Harper Collins.
Lawler, E.E., & Worley, C.G. (2009). Designing organizations that are built to change. In *The organization of the future 2:*

Visions, strategies, and insights on managing in a new era (eds Hessenlbein, F. & Goldsmith, M.). Chapter 16. San Francisco, CA: Jossey-Bass.

Lewin, A.Y., Long, C.P. & Timothy, N.C. (1999). The coevolution of new organizational forms. *Organization Science*, 10 (5): 535–550.

Lewin, A.Y., & Volberda, H.W. (1999). Prolegomena on coevolution: A framework for research on strategy and new organizational forms. *Organization Science*, 10 (5): 519–534.

Loch, C.H., Sting, F.J., Bauer, N. & Mauermann, H. (2010). The Globe: How BMW is defusing the demographic time bomb. *Harvard Business Review*, March 1: 99–102.

Lockwood, N. (2003). The aging workforce: The reality of the impact of older workers and eldercare in the workplace. *HR Magazine* (Business section). December. Accessed at http://findarticles.com/p/articles/mi_m3495/is_12_48/ai_n5989579/?tag=content;col1.

Lombardo, M.M. & Eichinger, R. (2001). *The Leadership Machine: Architecture to Develop Leaders for Any Future.* Minneapolis: Lominger International.

Magnuson, D.S., & Alexander, L.S. (2008). *Work with me. A new lens on leading the multigenerational workforce.* eBook. Minneapolis, MN: Personnel Decision.

Mallon, M. (1998). From managerial career to portfolio career: Making sense of the transition. Unpublished PhD thesis. Sheffield Hallam University.

Malone, T.W. (2004). *The future of work.* Boston, MA: Harvard Business School Press.

Malone, T.W., Laubacher, R. & Scott Morton, M.S. (2003). *Inventing the organizations of the 21st century.* Cambridge, MA: MIT Press.

Manpower (2009). The power of employment value proposition. A Manpower white paper. A publication of Manpower Services (Australia). https://www.manpowerprofessional.co.nz/Documents/White-Papers/2009_EVP%20White%20Paper.pdf.

Manyika, J., Lund, S., Auguste, B., Mendoca, L., Welsh, T. & Ramaswamy, S. (2011). An economy that works: Job creation and America's future. McKinsey Global Institute (MGI) report. http://www.google.com/url?sa=t&rct=j&q =&esrc=s&frm=1&source=web&cd=3&ved=0CEUQFjA C&url=http%3A%2F%2Fwww.mckinsey.com%2F~%2 Fmedia%2FMcKinsey%2Fdotcom%2FInsights%2520and% 2520pubs%2FMGI%2FResearch%2FLabor%2520Markets% 2FAn%2520economy%2520that%2520works%2520 Job%2520creation%2520and%2520Americas%2520future% 2FMGI_US_job_creation_full_report.ashx&ei=W0rHULi8 G8WBiwKrmoHgCQ&usg=AFQjCNH7fIwGMhlO5tzHBg 3wFoPsKiHprw&sig2=3TXBAh_7EwJI47iG_hOrpg&bvm= bv.1354675689,d.cGE.

Martin, C.A. (2005). From high maintenance to high productivity: What managers need to know about Generation Y. *Industrial and Commercial Training*, 37 (1): 39–44.

Martin, C.A., & Tulgan, B. (2006). *Managing the generation mix*. From urgency to opportunity. Amherst, Mass: HRD Press, Inc.

McCarthy, D. (2009). The leader of the future: Ten skills to begin developing now. Accessed at http://www.iabc.com/ cwb/archive/2009/0509/McCarthy.htm.

McGuire, D., Todnem, R.B. & Hutchings, K. (2007). Towards a model of human resource solutions for achieving intergenerational interaction in organisations. *Journal of European Industrial Training*, 31 (8): 592–608.

Meister, J.C., & Willyerd, K. (2010). *The 2020 workplace. How innovative companies attract, develop, and keep tomorrow's employees today*. New York: Harper Collins.

Morrison, J.L. (1992). Environmental scanning. In *A primer for new institutional researchers* (eds White, M.A., Porter, J.D. & Fenske, R.H.). pp 86–99. Tallahassee, FL: Association for Institutional Research.

Peters, T.J., & Waterman, R.H. (1982). In *Search of excellence. Lessons from America's best-run companies*. New York: Warner Books.

Pettigrew, A.M., & Fenton, E.M. (2000). *The innovating organization*. London: Sage.
Pettigrew, A.M., & Whipp, R. (1991). *Managing change for competitive success*. Oxford, UK: Blackwell Oxford.
Pettigrew, A.M., Whittington, R., Melin, L., Sánchez-Runde, C., van den Bosch, F., Ruigrok, W. & Numagami, T. (2003). *Innovative forms of organizing*. London: Sage.
Quam, K.F. (2010). The mature workforce and the changing nature of work. In *Research in organizational change and development*. Volume 18, pp. 315–366 (eds Pasmore, W.A., Shani, A.B. & Woodman, R.W.). Bingley, UK: Emerald.
Rindova, V.P., & Kotha, S. (2001). "Continuous morphing": Competing through dynamic capabilities, form, and function. *Academy of Management Journal*, 44 (6), 1263–1280.
Robertson, T.S., & Wind, Y. (1983). Organizational cosmopolitanism and innovativeness. *Academy of Management Journal*, 26 (2): 332–338.
Romanelli, E., & Tushman, M.L. (1994). Organizational transformation as punctuated equilibrium: An empirical test. *Academy of Management Journal*, 37 (5): 1141–1166.
Roth, A.V. (1996). Achieving strategic agility through economics of knowledge. *Strategy and Leadership*, 24 (2): 30–36.
Salkowitz, R. (2008). *Generation blend. Managing across the technology age gap*. Hoboken, NJ: John Wiley.
Sandulli, F.D., & Chesbrough, H. (2009). Open business models: The two sides of open business models. *Universia Business Review*, 2: 12–39.
Schmidt, S.R., & Svorny, S.V. (1998). Recent trends in job security and stability. *Labor Research*, 19 (4): 647–668.
Shafer, R.A. (1999). Only the agile will survive. *HR Magazine*, 44 (11): 50–51.
Shapero, M.A. (2012). Managing China's Millennials: Considerations for multinationals. Working Paper. January 2012. Florida: Eckerd College. Accessed at http://www.eckerd.edu/academics/internationalbusiness/files/china_research12.pdf.

Smith, B., & Raspin, P. (2011). *Creating market insight: How firms create value from market understanding*. San Francisco, CA: John Wiley.

Sujansky, J.G., & Ferri-Reed, J. (2009). *Keeping the Millennials. Why companies are losing billions in turnover to this generation – and what to do about it.* Hoboken, NJ: John Wiley.

Tapscott, D. (2009). *Grown up digital. How the net generation is changing your world.* New York: McGraw-Hill.

Terjesen, S., & Viola-Frey, R. (2008). Attracting and retaining Generation Y knowledge worker talent. In Smart Talent Management. Edited by Vaiman, V. & Vance, C.M (2008). pages 66–90. Cheltenham: Edward Elgar Publishing.

Tower, W. (2010) Global Workforce Study Reports: How far, how fars and how ending, New York, USA.

Tushman, M.L., & Scalan, T.J. (1981). Boundary spanning individuals: Their role in information transfer and their antecedents. *Academy of Management Journal*, 24 (2): 289–305.

Van Dam, N. (2011). *Next learning, unwrapped.* eBook. Raleigh N.C: Lulu Publishers.

Volberda, H.W. (1999). *Building the flexible firm.* Oxford, UK: Oxford University Press.

Volberda, H.W., Baden-Fuller, C. & van den Bosch, F.A.J. (2001). Mastering strategic renewal: Mobilising renewal journeys in multi-unit firms. *Long Range Planning*, 34, 159–178.

Ward, C. (1994). What is agility? *IIE Solutions*, 26 (11): 14–15.

Waterman, R., Peters, T.J., & Phillips, J.R. (1980). Structure is not organization. *Business Horizons*, 23 (3): 14–26.

Webb, D.L., & Pettigrew, A.M. (1999). The temporal development of strategy: Patterns in the UK insurance industry. *Organization Science*, 10 (5): 601–621.

Wideman, L. (1998). Alliances and networks: The next generation. *International Journal of Technology Management*, 15 (½): 96–108.

Wiersema, M.F., & Bantel, K.A. (1992). Top management team demography and corporate strategic change. *Academy of Management Journal*, 35 (1), 91–121.

Index of Companies and Organizations

Accenture, 45, 55, 71, 73, 106
Accordion Partners, 6, 134
Aditya Birla, 86
ASIAM Business Group, 52
AES, 5, 67, 74
AGD, 6, 157, 158
Amazon, 18, 66
Ambev, 65
AMC Theatres, 6, 86
Apple, 65, 66

Banco do Brazil, 65
Banco Itaú, 65
Bertelsmann, 72
Berkshire Hathaway, 66
Best Buy, 6, 133, 150
BMW, 5, 41, 42
Boston Consulting Group, 65–6
British Petroleum, 6, 107, 108

Canada Revenue Agency, 65
Cirque du Soleil, 5, 46, 47
Cisco, 89, 133
Cliff Bar & Co, 6
Coca-Cola, 66
Coty, 5, 74–8

Deloitte, 5, 51, 53–4, 65, 71–4
Dow, 6, 88, 89

ebay, 18
elBulli, 7, 31–4

Eli Lilly & Co, 17
Ernst & Young, 65, 82

FC Barcelona, 141, 142, 144
Facebook, 16, 17, 45, 65, 82, 84, 85, 99, 102, 125
FBI, 65
FedEx, 66, 93
Flickr, 18, 82
Ford, 11
Fotolog, 18
Frisse Blikken, 7, 58, 59, 60, 61

General Electric, 128
Genetech, 139
Google, 14, 18, 65, 66, 101
Government of Canada, 65

Hi5, 18, 82, 84

IBM, 13, 50
Infosys, 47, 49
InnoCentive, 16, 17

JetBlue, 133

La Masía, 7, 141–4
Lastminute.com, 6, 108, 109, 110
Lavazza, 32
Lays, 32
LinkedIn, 18, 82, 83, 84, 85

Lockheed Martin Company, 139
L'Oréal, 6, 7, 63, 70, 83, 84, 90, 92, 95, 96, 97, 98, 151

McKinsey, 65, 66, 146
Motorola, 86
msm.com, 18
MySpace, 18, 45, 82

Natura, 6, 154–6
Nestlé, 86
NH Hotels, 32

Oil Spill Recovery Institute, 17

Pandora, 82
Paypal.com, 18
Peace Corps, 5, 70–1
Pepsico, 32
Pernod Ricard, 6, 122, 124
Petrobras, 65
Pricewaterhouse and Coopers, 66, 71
Procter & Gamble, 13

Rabobank, 6, 117, 118

Salesforce.com, 5, 69
Second Life, 45, 84
Sodexo, 6, 83, 84, 85
Solvay, 17
Southwest Airlines, 66

Tata, 73
Teach for America, 5, 68, 69
Threadless, 5, 15, 16, 24
Twitter, 16, 18, 82, 83, 85, 86, 102

Vale, 65

Walt Disney Company, 65
Wikipedia, 5, 14–15, 18, 101

Yahoo!, 18, 110
Youtube, 18, 82, 85, 101, 102

Zappo, 6, 86

Subject Index

Careers
  boundaryless, 10, 130, 140
  customized portfolio career, 10, 136, 137, 140
  enhancement, 131, 135
  and flexible work, 10, 135
  and HR practices, 138
  lattice, 129, 130, 131, 139
  mass career customization, 10, 135
  portfolio, 10, 130, 131, 136

Demographic change
  and the aging workforce, 38, 41, 42
  baby boomers, 35–40, 43, 47, 51
  and differences between generations, 8, 51
  generation X, 36
  generation Z, 36
  and generational clashes, 49
  and main features throughout different generations, 36–8, 39
  overlapping generations and, 35, 42–3, 49
  traditionalists, 36–40, 53
  worldwide, 38, 46, 50–5

Employee Value Proposition (EVP)
  aspects of an
  social impact of the job, 9, 75
  the "me brand", 75, 77
  window to the world, 70, 75
  and branding, 64
  building an, 63
  definition of, 64

Leaders of the future
  activities for developing the, 120
  the capacity of learning, unlearning and renewal of the, 10
  collaboration skills of the, 122
  developing the, 99–144
  dimensions for, 114, 120
  and interpersonal competencies, 120
  and managerial competencies, 118
  managing the, 118, 121–4
  and new competencies, 115, 124

Millennials (also Generation Y or Gen Y)
  and the agile and virtual firm, 44
  attracting, 63–98
  characteristics, 48, 74, 75, 103, 123, 131, 132–3
  and the critical role of technology, 113
  and multitasking preference, 8, 44, 45, 75, 103, 123, 132

Millennials (also Generation Y or Gen Y) – *continued*
  and new cosmopolitans, 55
  and new ways of organizing, 47
  and organizational implications, 48, 132–3
  and their social consciousness, 44
  and work–life integration, 44, 46, 48, 75, 103, 123, 132

New learning paradigms
  education system and, 53, 100
  formal learning and, 102, 104, 106
  individual learning and, 101, 106
  informal learning and, 104
  organizational learning and, 101, 102
  social learning and, 102, 104
  a strategy for supporting, 105
  teaching Millennials and, 123
  and workplace learning, 100, 102

New ways of organizing
  and crowdsourcing, 14, 16
  and decentralization, 12, 13
  and inertia, 9, 12
  and innovation and agility, 10, 12
  and knowledge-based organizations, 30
  and open business systems, 47
  and organizational complexity, 147
  and organizational effectiveness, 145, 147, 157
  and organizational health, 147, 148, 163
  and virtual organizations (virtuality), 12

Organizational agility
  and alignment, 147
  and coherence, 160
  definition, 22
  determinants, 8, 22
  and fast responsiveness, 161
  and innovation, 160
  managerial determinants of, 19
  a model of
    new cognitive diversity, 149–50
    new HR paradigms, 153–6
    fast anticipatory capacity, 150–3
    strong sense of purpose, 156–61
  organizational determinants of, 8

Recruitment
  new approach, 82
    being a coach of your candidates, 9
    being aggressive and persuasive on benefits, 9, 82, 85
    being social, 9, 82
  strategy, 81, 82
  and technology, 81

Social networks
  and recruiting, 81–94
  use of internet and, 17, 45, 81, 108

MIX
Papier aus verantwortungsvollen Quellen
Paper from responsible sources
FSC® C105338

If you have any concerns about our products,
you can contact us on
ProductSafety@springernature.com

In case Publisher is established outside the EU,
the EU authorized representative is:
**Springer Nature Customer Service Center GmbH
Europaplatz 3, 69115 Heidelberg, Germany**

Printed by Libri Plureos GmbH
in Hamburg, Germany